One
Nation
Under a
Groove

One
Nation
Under a
Groove

Motown and American Culture

by Gerald Early

The Ecco Press

Copyright © 1995 by Gerald Early

The Ecco Press
100 West Broad Street
Hopewell, New Jersey 08525
Published simultaneously in Canada by
Penguin Books Canada Ltd., Ontario
Printed in the United States of America

Designed by Richard Oriolo

FIRST EDITION

Library of Congress Cataloging-in-Publication Data

Early, Gerald Lyn.
One nation under a groove : Motown and American culture /
by Gerald Early.—1st ed.
p.   cm.
ISBN 0-88001-379-6
1. Motown Record Corporation. 2. Sound recording
industry—United States. I. Title.
ML3792.E27 1995
306.4'84—dc20   94-43647

The text of this book is set in Horley Old Style

To Mr. Lloyd Richard King,
my teacher,
who always believed in me.
Would that I were always worthy
of that great faith.

Contents

Introduction / 1

I. **Family Happiness** / 9

II. **A Usable Black Present or the Lessons of Booker T. Washington and Joe Louis** / 35

III. **The Midwest as Musical Mecca and the Rise of Rhythm and Blues** / 67

IV. **The Shrine and the Seer** / 107

Introduction

In recent years, as I became more and more identified as someone with expertise in popular culture or with an intellectual predisposition toward popular culture and its study, I grew more wary of both the subject and my association with it. I could think of nothing I wanted less than such an identification; not, as it were, that this disinclination was the outgrowth of any sort of dislike of the subject or the squeamishness connected with the act of being exposed at "slumming," after all. That some of my colleagues might feel the subject to be something of an indulgence or a squandering of time and talent that can rightly be traced to Rousseau having come into the world is not, frankly, a major worry, as I never wholly believed myself to be a guardian of the culture, although I am by no means bashful about enjoying the perks and privileges, the overall sense of cultivation, of being part of an elite. My interest in popular culture does not generate from so vainglorious and heroic a source as the need to identify with the working classes or the masses, nor as an expression of contempt against the status conferred upon high culture. I am not so childishly egalitarian as that, or as the working-class and poor boys with whom I grew up used to put it when fiercely competing on the playground, "If you want my respect, you gotta earn it." Besides, to paraphrase an old saw, I've been working class and I've been middle class and middle class is better, taken all around, even if to earn someone's respect these days all I have to do primarily is be willing to buy it.

Rather, I have felt as if such an identification with popular culture were not, to use a phrase, "truth in advertising." My interest in popular culture is narrow, almost to the point of being a small series of points, perhaps of light, but surely not as benighted as some might think: namely, boxing, baseball, boys' literature at the turn of the century, and jazz. This list seems to take modesty to a new depth of complete unassumingness. (And I might add that I have so assiduously avoided the possible taint of "expertise" that I have never considered teaching any of these subjects as courses; that would strike me as being both bizarre and unintelligible.) I never wanted to be one of those intellectuals who hung around kitsch because it was hip, easy to write about, and, with a cynical mixture of appreciation and gratitude, easy to make a reputation with because one was destined, in writing about it, always to sound smarter than the subject at hand. With varying degrees of interest I read theories about popular culture (of which there are no small number) and the political interpretations these theories suggest. I have never been interested in constructing any of my own, although some might suppose this book makes gestures in that direction. I will explain to them that the book is a "meditation on," not a "theory about."

Motown, the subject of this small book, was never a passion of mine. I appreciate the music, am deeply fond of much of it, but I was not driven to write about it simply from a nostalgic urge (the most sentimental and often misguided corruption of both the past and the present) to talk about a popular music with which I grew up. A hazard lurked, as real as the romanticization of personal memory, behind the allure of writing about something so closely associated with growing up, of being drawn to it simply because one is, naturally, drawn with pain and pleasure to one's childhood and adolescence. Something else, larger and more dispassionately demanding, was what had to be pursued here. There were other matters I wished to tackle in looking at Motown, specifically about African-American life and culture in the 1950s, 1960s, and 1970s, not fully explored but tentatively mapped out for fuller exploration in some future book or two. Indeed, I see this brief effort as something like a prelude and fugue to some deeper studies that— imagining them as something like grand symphonies— would be attractive to fewer readers, if only because, wishing to aspire to greater invention, they run a greater risk of being such utter failures.

Leon Wieseltier of the *New Republic* approached me a few years ago to write an article on Motown. I would never have thought of it myself and indeed had never thought about it until the very moment of being challenged by Mr. Wieseltier's offer. Why he approached me I do not know, unless he too saw me as something like a pop culture guy or perhaps a music guy since I had written some pieces about jazz or perhaps a polemics guy since I am black. (In the case of pop culture, I certainly

3

do not put myself in the class of, say, Nelson George, or in the case of jazz writing, in the class of Stanley Crouch, or in the case of polemics, in the class of, say, Ralph Wiley or Thomas Sowell or bell hooks. I am compelled by modesty and sheer common sense to make that small confession so that, as sometimes happens in this society, I am not confused with any other black man or woman who writes for a living; there being, to use Moses' phrase, undeniably, "a confusion of tongues" among African-Americans.) What was ultimately published in the pages in that magazine was perhaps 60 to 70 percent of the original manuscript, although as Mr. Wieseltier reassured me through his competent editing, the final published version, basically maintaining the integrity of the original, was among the longer pieces that the *New Republic* ever published.

This book is, in fact, much closer to what I had in mind when I finished the piece for Mr. Wieseltier, a miniepic meditation on two ideas. The first is that Motown was important because it helped to crystallize the formation, not of a black audience (that had existed before), but of a black public and a black public taste that was taken seriously as an expression of a general aesthetic among a broad class of Americans. The creation of a black public—a body of black folk who have no connection with each other or commitment to each other except the idea that they are consumers whose consumption is given meaning because of their race— is, I think, a very different abstraction from the idea of

4

a black community. Second, Motown, an extraordinary success in the realm of mass culture or popular culture, actually helped to bring into clear definition the taste and urges of a middle-brow black audience whose existence helped to create such middle-brow black conceptions as Afrocentrism, the name African-American, and the mythology of the black community. Jazz had been, until the 1950s, a middle-brow music of Broadway tunes and blues-based improvisations that suddenly turned into a high-brow expression when it became self-consciously obsessed by all varieties of *composition* and completely left the realm of popular dance, leaving a void in African-American culture that was filled nicely by Motown.

In short, it is my hope that I might have more to say about Motown than that it was a successful black record company, a successful black business, or that, alas, white folk liked the music. This last point, in some measure, seems to me to be especially trivial as whites were always admirers of black music and have always, for some reason, felt compelled to make a histrionic point of it. That Motown was the soundtrack for *The Big Chill* seems less important than the fact that it was the soundtrack for *Nothing But a Man*, a film that may be more important for all of our children in the long run. But then again, I am much of the mind that Alan Freed's cheap, awful rock-and-roll "documentaries" are of greater significance in talking about miscegenation than, say, *Blackboard Jungle*, our first rock-and-roll film, as it is commonly called. It is my hope that most of this or, at least, some of it, will be made a bit clearer here than it may have been in the piece as it was printed in the *New Republic*.

I would like to thank Dan Halpern for asking me to write this book and Mr. Wieseltier for having made it possible. I want to thank my wife, Ida, and our daughters, Linnet and Rosalind, for having put up with so many hours of hearing me talk about Motown and for so many hours of listening to Motown records. This last, though, was not so bad as all that and everyone always wound up singing and dancing the night away.

Finally, I would like to thank Theo Broughton, a fine woman, without whose generous assistance I would not have been able to complete the original *New Republic* article or this book.

Straight Ahead   St. Louis, Missouri
Gerald Early   August 8, 1994

One
Nation
Under a
Groove

Family

Happiness

One generation passeth away . . .

How can, Oh, how can those enemies but say that we and
our children are not of the HUMAN FAMILY . . .

—David Walker's *Appeal to the Colored Citizens
of the World*

My dream was to become Frank Sinatra. I loved his
phrasing, especially when he was very young and pure. He
grew into a fabulous jazz singer and I used to fantasize
about having a lifestyle like his—carrying on in
Hollywood and becoming a movie star. Every woman in
America wanted to go to bed with Frank Sinatra. He was
the king I longed to be. My greatest dream was to satisfy
as many women as Sinatra. He was the heavyweight
champ, the absolute.
Now this is going to surprise you, but I also dug Dean
Martin and especially Perry Como. They weren't monster
singers, but I liked their relaxed presentation. Perry had a
great attitude. When I finally got some money together
over at Motown in the sixties, I used to sport Perry
Como's sweaters. I always felt like my personality and
Perry's had a lot in common.

—Marvin Gaye, from David Ritz's *Divided Soul: The Life of
Marvin Gaye*

This organization is built on love.

—Berry Gordy, Jr. about Motown, *Newsweek,* March 22, 1965

The African-American and the Italian

It is one of the peculiar and penetrating gestures of "crossover" in American culture that in the 1960s, Marvin Gaye could fantasize about being an Italian pop ballad singer, making four ballads-and-standards albums for Motown between 1961 and 1965, while Felix Cavaliere, Italian lead singer of the Rascals, could fantasize about being a black soul singer with such songs for Atlantic as "Good Lovin' " (1966) and "Groovin' " (1967), which topped the R and B charts. This fantasy-swapping-cum-mutual-admiration seems an old business with blacks and Italians in music: The legendary guitarist Eddie Lang was born Salvatore Massaro and often recorded under the name of Blind Willie Dunn, as if he were a black country musician. On the other hand, bass saxophonist Adrian Rollini had no bigger admirers than Coleman Hawkins and Harry Carney, and there was the great black opera star of the 19th century, Thomas Bowers, who was called "The Colored Mario" because he sounded so much like Italian tenor Giovanni Mario.

Considering the blatant sexual nature of most popular American dance music ("We're selling sex," Paul Williams reminded his fellow Temptations as they donned their form-fitting trousers), both Gaye and Cavaliere betrayed a kind of sexual envy of the other's ethnic identity. A strange affair for two ethnic groups that never liked one another very well. For example, the Detroit race riot of 1942, fought, in part, over the issue of housing and leisure space, was largely, though not exclusively, a conflict between blacks and Italians. No matter how that may have turned out, certainly blacks thought when middleweight champion Sugar Ray Robinson flattened Rocky Graziano in three rounds in Chicago in 1952 that some score between the two groups had just been evened. They remembered, for example, when Dodger outfielder Carl Furillo and third baseman Cookie Lavagetto signed a petition in 1947, along with some die-hard southerners, saying that they would never play on the same team as Jackie Robinson. More recently, the first three of Sylvester Stallone's *Rocky* movies have exploited the conflict between blacks and Italians to great box-office advantage.

In the beginning of the fifties and well into the middle years of that decade, Italian male pop-crooners and melodramatic operatic tenors ruled popular music: Julius La Rosa, Al Martino, Dean Martin, Tony Bennett, Vic Damone, Mario Lanza, Frankie Laine, Jerry Vale, and Perry Como. The reigning prince was, of course, Frank Sinatra. The 1950s witnessed two major shifts in popular music: first, a movement away from the Tin Pan Alley–type popular songs of the Berlin-Gershwin-Arlen ilk to a music that was more obviously and overtly influenced by, and openly mimicked, black Rhythm and Blues; second, a shift away from middle-aged or mature-sounding Italian male singers as kings of the popular roost toward white Southerners, adolescent Jewish songwriters, and blacks as the trendsetters in popular music, a major ethnic shift that had a profound impact on the culture at large.

By the very early 1960s there were still several Italian male singers who, as teen idols, figured prominently in the "new music" called Rock and Roll: Bobby Rydell and Frankie Avalon (both discovered by Paul Whiteman, the WASP bandleader-turned-personality disc jockey, and purveyor of symphonic jazz in the 1920s, who was known in his heyday as "The King of Jazz"), Bobby Darin, Fabian, Frankie Valli of the Four Seasons, Joey Dinicola of Joey Dee and the Starliters, and Dion DiMucci of Dion and the Belmonts. Despite their success, these acts were not the major forces in pop music that the Italian singers in the 1950s had been. Herein lies our tale: The two most successful of the Italian Rock and Roll brigade of the early sixties, Frankie Valli and the Four Seasons on the one hand and Bobby Darin on the other, are the Alpha and Omega representations of the shift in popular music. The Four Seasons were originally signed by and recorded their first three million–selling hits for Vee Jay Records, a Chicago-based, largely (though by no means exclusively) Rhythm and Blues company, owned by blacks. Bobby Darin made his last album in 1972 for Motown Records, the most successful independent record company and the most successful black-owned business in American history. What follows is one story—of Frank Sinatra and the Great Displacement in American pop-culture mythology.

Because the election of John Kennedy, for whom Frank Sinatra campaigned ardently, was touted as a new beginning, the force with which the 1960 Frank Sinatra film *Ocean's 11* announced, ironically, the end of an era, is all the more striking, surrounded as that film is by a kind of modernistic despair. The fifties had been a strange decade for Sinatra—the years of his most profound career defeats and his most startling career triumphs. Among the negatives were the messy divorce from his first wife, Nancy; the much-publicized love affair with Ava Gardner, who became his second wife; the economic downfall of the big-band era after World War II—the era that had made Sinatra a "teen" or bobbysoxer star and shaped his aesthetic vision; the subsequent downturn in Sinatra's record sales, which resulted in his being dropped by the most prestigious of all American record companies, Columbia, in 1952; and the box-office failure of the 1952 film *Meet Danny Wilson* (actually, one of his more peculiar formulaic films from the early period), after all of which Sinatra seemed irretrievably on the skids. How the Academy Award–winning role of

Maggio in the 1953 film *From Here to Eternity* and the 1953 contract with Capitol, the only record company at the time that had even a remote interest in Sinatra, revived his career is now well known. Sinatra went on to become a major box-office attraction in the 1950s, and his Capitol records are now considered perhaps his best work; they certainly reestablished him as king of the pop hill. He sold more records in the 1950s than any other artist, finally managing to replace, in fact and as icon, Bing Crosby, as American's greatest pop singer (although, to be sure, Crosby still sold well). Sinatra became, without question, at this time, the most magnetic Italian presence in American popular culture, eclipsing even the Yankee Clipper, Joe DiMaggio, despite DiMaggio's brief marriage to Marilyn Monroe—one of the stranger celebrity unions—and his incredible success at being able to remain nothing more (or less) than Joe DiMaggio from the day he retired on December 11, 1951.

After the death in 1957 of Humphrey Bogart, a man he greatly admired, Sinatra became the head of the Rat Pack, also called the Clan, an influential nonconformist group of the Hollywood hip that included Dean Martin, Sammy Davis, Jr., Judy Garland, Peter Lawford, Lauren Bacall, Debbie Reynolds, Shirley MacLaine, Joey Bishop, Billy Wilder, and Sammy Cahn and Jimmy Van Heusen (virtually Sinatra's personal songwriters, who penned several Academy Award–winning or nominated hits for his films of the 1950s, including "The Tender Trap," "All the Way," "High Hopes," and "The Second Time Around"). It was the famous Hollywood family of playboys and playgirls, of ethnic outcasts—Italians (Sinatra, Martin), Jews (Cahn, Bishop), blacks (Davis, who was also a Jew)—whose inclusive exclusivity (No Squares, Finks, Mice, or Losers Need Apply!) was an ironic commentary on the racial bigotry or exclusive inclusivity of the Ku Klux Klan, a hate group revived in the heat of the civil rights movement of the 1950s whose victims were largely blacks, Jews, and Italians, and other Catholics. (As Ralph Abernathy commented during the 1965 Selma march, "The only ones they hate more than Negroes down here are Roman Catholics. . . .")

Sinatra had, in fact, established a white, liberal onscreen persona in the 1958 Delmer Daves World War II film *Kings Go Forth,* where he played a working-class sergeant in France who falls in love with Natalie Wood, who, he learns, is biracial, the daughter of a white mother and black father. The Sinatra character, at first, experiences a moment of prejudice but so loves Wood that he overcomes it. She does not feel a sexual attraction toward him. Tony Curtis—ironically, since he is Jewish—plays a rich WASP soldier, a jazz player and charmer, who has a momentary dalliance with Wood but devastates her when he abandons her, unable and, more important, unwilling, to overcome his racism. The film is particularly frank and undoubtedly shocking for its day in having Wood's mother talk about her passionate love for a black man, her late husband, and how they were unable to live in the United States with their child. (The film suggests, among other things, that miscegenation is impossible to acknowledge in America which, one supposes, many black American expatriates already knew.) *Kings Go Forth* generally was in keeping with the kind of problem-of-race film that was being made at the time. Indeed, Wood's tragic mulatto character was a throwback to something like the first *Imitation of Life* film in 1934, except that it was more convincing to hear the late Freddie Washington, a light-skinned Negro, in the adaptation of the Fannie Hurst novel, say she was ashamed of being black than it was to hear Wood, a white, say in *Kings Go Forth* that she was proud of being a Negro!

In part, Sinatra's liberalism may be a direct outgrowth of his association with swing music, specifically, and jazz, generally, music that tended to emphasize the democratic impulses of the culture within a strict system of meritocracy. It might be accurately said that the swing-music era was racist, with white bands getting most of the publicity and money. (It must be noted here that Sinatra has made records with the two major black jazz bands of American popular-music history, Count Basie and Duke Ellington, where both black band leaders were given equal billing with him.) Nonetheless, several black swing bands did reasonably well during the 1930s and 1940s, and, more important, popular music in America became openly integrated both on record and in public performance during this time. Jazz, in its relentless professionalism, encouraged, even created, a plural-istic elite, as Lewis A. Erenberg notes: ". . . swing was profoundly cosmopolitan, including blacks, Jews, Italians, Poles, Irish, and Protestant leaders, players, and singers." In some sense, the Rat Pack, the Clan, resem-bled the pluralistic impulse of the swing music that Sinatra has never ceased to love.

Despite his enormous success and power in the fifties, Sinatra was witnessing, in the arena of popular culture where hipness was being defined anew, the very elements of his own demise as a force due to the sheer inescapable fact that he was too old to be hip any longer. The very same inchoate structure of the youth culture that made him a pop success in the 1940s—mostly, though not en-tirely, made up of adolescent white girls (Shirley Temple's mediocre 1942 film, *Miss Annie Rooney,* in which she played a working-class teenager in love with big bands, revealed that teenaged girls were already a force as a popular music audience long before Rock and Roll appeared)—were to declare him irrelevant by 1960. As *Life* magazine wrote in a 1958 article on the Clan, Sinatra was more than the "reigning social monarch," "the prophet" of a new social order in Hollywood. He was the "angry middle-aged man," and, in the light of the rise of Rhythm and Blues and Rock and Roll, he became the first and most public of Americans of this age to have a temper tantrum about becoming old when so much of his appeal was based on a youth and hipness that had passed him by.

Ocean's 11, a misogynistic hallucination featuring
the extended Rat Pack or Clan—Sinatra, Davis, Martin,
Lawford, Bishop, Henry Silva, and Richard Conte, as
well as women fellow travelers, Angie Dickin-son and
MacLaine—tells the tale of eleven ex–World War II
paratroopers who band together to rob five Las Vegas
casinos with a bit of ingenuity and derring-do. The film
is actually a paean of old-style masculine hip by the family to itself, but it seems to lack both energy and sincer-
ity. Sinatra and his friends, in a film that seems like an in-
fantile frat-house joke, are engaged in a sort of last gasp,
the final ideological assault of old-fashioned swing—an
oxymoronic virtue of "cool" indulgence—against the
hedonistic decadence and nihilism of the era of Rock and
Roll. These slightly overaged playboys, exhibiting all the
symptoms of a midlife crisis, decide to turn back the
clock and become adventurers again as they had been in
the army. The fact that Sinatra himself and most of the
Clan's major players, such as Martin and Lawford, never
served in the army, and the fact that it would have been
impossible for Sammy Davis—who did actually serve in
the armed forces—to have been in the same outfit with
the others during World War II, inasmuch as the army
was segregated, are curious and telling fantasies and
anachronisms.

When the men gather around a pool table—that sign
of a tough, working-class boyhood and of the hip, masculine adult as a hustling "adept"—to discuss their plans
for robbing Las Vegas, a strange note of confession is

sounded when Dean Martin's character criticizes the whole enterprise:

I like to swing like the rest of you guys but you haven't got a plan here, you've got a pipeload. This ain't a combat team, it's an alumni meeting.

He further elaborates when Sinatra's character, Danny Ocean, asks him what is wrong with the plan:

For one thing . . . fifteen years. Any of you liars want to claim you're half the man you were in '45? Can you run as fast? Can you think as fast? Can you mix it up as good as you used to? Well, I sure can't. And Danny, if you want to try to catch lightning in a bottle, you go ahead. But don't try to catch yesterday. Old times are only good when you've had 'em.

Martin's words are not heeded by the others and he himself finally falls in line and the story proceeds. It is the film's sincerest moment; the rest, after it is decided to proceed with this perverse rumination, is tripe in the name of revolt against the new order.

Oddly, in the screenplay about robbing casinos, the Pack gives the impression of biting the hand that feeds them, as they were all well-known Vegas lounge acts. But once again, there is the air of this being something of an inside joke. It is well to remember that after World War II, with Vegas the gambling capital of America and the coming in 1955 of Disneyland, the most famous theme park in history, capital investment was concentrated in the West, creating, in essence, playgrounds for adults and children, hedonistic spaces that juxtaposed the fantasy of wholesome, bourgeois fun for the family (American pietism) with the fantasy of getting rich without effort and a sybarite lifestyle (American sin). All of this simultaneously was, if not a new order itself, then perhaps a determined reactionism to uphold the status quo, which in America constantly needs to be rescued from the taint of modernity—even as, in the case of Las Vegas and Disneyland, they genuflect, in their invention, to this extravagantly abundant modernity—as an act of homage to the glories of the past. It might be said that the film, in its confusion, was an attack against a certain manifestation of mass culture by people who had been made possible by it.

The shadow that looms over *Ocean's 11,* that provoked Martin's moment of honesty, that very unexpectedly aged the nonconformist congeries of white hipsters of the 1950s—from Mailer to Sinatra, from the Beat to the Pack—into a kind of outraged and bewildered, threatened and uneasy establishment, was Rock and Roll, which seemed to conjure forth even more miscegenation, unbridled and puerile, unsettling and more egalitarian, than the hipness of jazz, now stodgy and high-hat, could ever have envisioned.

  Basically, rock 'n' roll—which has little musical eloquence—is a singer's highly personal way of shouting

or moaning lyrics ("The Big Sound"), mostly to a slow,
heavily accentuated four-four time ("The Big Beat"),
accompanied by guitar or hoarse-honked tenor
saxophone. It is eight years old but only in the past two or
three years has it proven that it is more than a flash in the
piano.

—"Rock 'N' Roll Rolls On 'N' On," *Life Magazine,*
December 22, 1958

In November 1957, a piece by Sinatra—entitled "The
Diplomacy of Music"—appeared in a magazine called
Western World. In it he juxtaposed the cool world of jazz
and the hip heat of Rock and Roll by discussing the State
Department-sponsored trips of jazzmen like trumpeters
Louis Armstrong, the "Uncle Tom-ish" old guard
Dixielander, and Dizzy Gillespie, the racially conscious
be-bopper, to the Middle East and Europe. As late as
1949, an editorial in *Ebony* magazine had stated: "The
long war between boppist and anti-boppist factions was
almost political in its defenses. Boppists likened themselves to revolutionary leftists, their opponents as
money-grabbing capitalists. Now, as the battle draws to
a close, boppists find themselves in a musical equivalent
of a political underground." That Armstrong and
Gillespie should be yoked together when they represented such different approaches to the art of improvisa-
tional music—indeed, approaches, no matter how rooted
in the blues or the pop song "standard," that were, to
some, political counterstatements to one another—is a
striking example of how acceptable and even respectable

jazz had become, despite the fact that Charlie Parker's highly publicized death had occurred just two years earlier and the drug-related deaths of Lester Young and Billie Holiday were to occur two years later. (Obviously, to send Armstrong and Gillespie abroad was to show the rest of the "colored world"—an all-too-real political specification in the anti–European colonialism world of 1950s Asia and Africa—that white America could revere two colored men and could, indeed, send them forth as practitioners of a respected, indigenous art form.)

In two of the most famous youth films of the 1950s, *Blackboard Jungle* and *Jailhouse Rock,* jazz was in fact portrayed as being virtually the property of "intellectuals," "teachers," "authority figures," almost a reactionary art form of egregious pretension. (It is only in a film like Alan Freed's *Mister Rock and Roll* that one sees the radical connection between jazz, Rhythm and Blues, and Rock and Roll in the figure of Lionel Hampton, in effect, the star of the movie—he begins and ends it—and the true Mr. Rock and Roll.) Like Sinatra himself, jazz had grown from its saloon origins to become both typical and representative of America:

> And good or bad, [jazz] causes millions of people outside the United States to believe that we are by no means as crude, mysterious or childish as our foreign policy or its representatives have more often than not caused them to believe. And for that reason alone we should treat it and its makers with constant respect and

admiration. That aspect of it to which I contribute is also a considerable force for good in that tasteful songs and musically competent orchestral backgrounds, whether the words are understood or not, help keep the door open.

But the defense of jazz—which in the 1910s and 1920s was called by many status quo critics "crude, mysterious, and childish"—comes at the expense of Rock and Roll, which Sinatra calls

> . . . the most brutal, ugly, degenerate, vicious form of expression it has been my displeasure to hear. . . . It fosters almost totally negative and destructive reactions in young people. It smells phony and false. It is sung, played and written for the most part by cretinous goons and by means of its almost imbecilic reiterations and sly, lewd, in fact plain dirty—lyrics . . . it manages to be the martial music of every sideburned delinquent on the face of the earth.

The obvious reference at the end to Elvis Presley, Sinatra's main rival in popular music from 1956 through the end of that decade (Presley had fifteen number-one pop hits between 1956 and 1960), is not simply over-wrought or excessively rehearsed; it is specifically generated by twin, conflicting urges in Sinatra: First, he uses the maniacal rhetoric of stigma and ridicule that historically had been used against Italians. ("Cretinous goons" and "most brutal, ugly, degenerate, vicious," were common descriptions of Italian gangsters and organized crime figures; "imbecilic reiterations" are suggestive of the implicit ridicule of Italian gestures and Pidgin English; even the "sideburned delinquent" conjures images of the "greaseball" with olive oil in his hair.) Second, the overheated critical language is nearly identical with that used to discredit ragtime at the turn of the century, jazz in its early days in the teens and twenties, and swing music of the thirties (Goodman at Carnegie Hall in 1938 was revolutionary)—musical forms that overturned prevailing notions and traditions in American popular music, which changed American popular dance, and which were rooted in African-American musical expression.

Sinatra was using the invectives that had once been directed at him as an Italian, an outcast minority, and as a product of swing music, a discredited art form, to denounce a new music he felt was about to displace him. His was the conservative's cry for standards—literally, in this case, as that is what the body of so-called "timeless" pop songs is called—by using the language of degradation and contempt that reveals nothing more tellingly than that the oppressed wish access to the measure of respectability and acceptance that will permit them the luxury of defending the status quo. Sinatra, the rebel against the Hollywood establishment, was really defending its virtues and values as the shaper—through film, radio, records, and music publishing by means of which the studios exercised their power in music—of the public's taste in popular music. But when Hollywood began making youth films and Presley films in the mid-1950s, it seemed no longer the bulwark against the mass infantilism and bad taste that was early Rock and Roll, according to many contemporary critics. It is no wonder he gathered the Clan—the family of Hollywood outsiders —to make *Ocean's 11,* a last psychoswing for masscult order and hipster resistance to another relentless surge of barbaric darkness in American life.

In 1959, the television series "The Untouchables" debuted much to the chagrin and displeasure of Sinatra and many other Italians, as they felt the show was defaming in its depiction of Prohibition-era Italian gangsters. Also in 1959, the federal government was investigating payola in radio air play, which resulted in the downfall of one popular Rock and Roll disc jockey, Alan Freed, but which also led to more insinuations about Italian gangsters in the pop music business. Earlier in the 1950s, a young Justice Department lawyer named Robert Kennedy had conducted an investigation of the teamsters' union and Jimmy Hoffa, which led to connections with organized crime and Italian gangsters. Boxing had also been investigated in the late 1950s, and while this exposure led to the downfall of the wealthy James Norris and his International Boxing Club, it also revealed that two Italian gangsters, Blinky Palermo and Frankie Carbo, were the masterminds behind restraint of trade and fixed fights in the boxing world.

Alan Freed's aforementioned self-serving and self-

mythologizing 1957 film, *Mister Rock and Roll,* is about
the rise of Teddy Randazzo, an Italian kid from New
York, drawn to black Rhythm and Blues, who becomes a
Rock and Roll singer, attracted to its sense of community, with Alan Freed as the father, as well to its aesthetics, but who is attacked in the respectable press for being
a "delinquent" and a "troublemaker" through his music.
Before Rock and Roll, he had worked as a bellhop in a
Cleveland hotel. Alan Freed saved him from a life of
working-class anonymity by bringing him together with
the other unwanteds: the blacks, both eastern and midwestern, southern hillbilly whites, Jewish novelty songwriters, the urban working-class white girl destined for
secretaryhood, all of whom make up his Rock and Roll
shows. (The stereotypical attack against the Italian
singer as a representative of his generation is not unlike
the stereotypical attack made against black youths today
and the music they are most identified with, Rap: "delin-
quents," "troublemakers," "degenerates," "gangsters.")
Ultimately, he and the girl reporter—who looks a great
deal like Grace Kelly, the blonde WASP princess every
ethnic male desires, and who inadvertently is responsible
for this attack—become lovers, and Rock and Roll suc-
ceeds against its reactionary critics. Miscegenation proceeds at its lightning pace, and the East Coast white ethnic is as much at the center as the white southern boy.
Oddly, the Italian, through his own ethnic darkness as
well as his association with the black, becomes a strange

figure of race mixing in America. Their own working-class fear of black competition in the job market and absorption of American racism made the Italians intensely anti-Negro, yet the Italian seems just a little better than a black, in the end. In passing, it is interesting to note one of the oddities of the American stage, the casting of a light-skinned black actor named Frank Silvera (who passed as a swarthy white but who, on several occasions, also played black roles) as the father of Italian actors Ben Gazzara and Tony Franciosa in *A Hatful of Rain.*

Sinatra was probably ambivalent about race mixing, supposedly having discouraged Sammy Davis, Jr., from marrying Kim Novak, with whom Davis had a love affair, but supporting him in his 1960 marriage to Swedish actress May Britt (a storm that Davis, with Sinatra's support, was able to weather a great deal better than Chubby Checker, the twist king, who, a few years later married a Scandinavian beauty queen and instantly disappeared from the charts). But Sinatra constantly made tasteless jokes about Sammy Davis's race and his interracial marriage during his 1960s stage act. The Italians had their Mafias, their Clans, their fixation on family, and their own fears of miscegenation, all of which made them so tribal. (While Sinatra had his Rat Pack, he also enjoyed tremendously the company of Italian gangsters and tough guys, a community which provided him, doubtless, with fantasy discharges about his masculinity and his ethnicity.) Perhaps Sinatra's ambiguity as Italian and aging pop singer was getting confused with and confronted by Rock and Roll's insistent myth of family togetherness.

Black Paternalism

In 1959, Berry Gordy, Jr., age 30, was forming his record company, Motown, or more precisely, Hitsville, U.S.A., in Detroit, built, at this early stage, primarily on the singing and songwriting strength of William "Smokey" Robinson, age 19, 1957 graduate of Northern High School, and Robinson's group, the Matadors, whom Gordy renamed the Miracles. (Robinson was always to hold a privileged position with the company. In the 1960s, he was the only performer who was permitted to write songs and produce recordings. He was also the only performer in the company's history to become a corporate executive.) The establishment of Motown was the beginning of a new family myth in popular culture, a myth that Motown has promoted and exploited for its entire history and has featured as a prominent part of its legacy. The 1985 film *The Big Chill,* which used Motown music as its soundtrack, was not only a sort of nostalgic memoir of a new "lost generation" but a coming together of people at a location to form a family. Virtually no major company in American history and surely no black company was ever so identified not simply as a family business but as a "family" enterprise for its employees; certainly, no independent record company was ever to manipulate so skillfully its humble, homemade origins as a mark of its distinction, its success, its power as a symbol in American culture in the way Motown has.

"By the time we returned in the winter of 1960, Motown was firmly established and running very much like family. Loyalty, honesty, and obedience were demanded and often gladly given," writes Mary Wilson of the Supremes in her autobiography, *Dream Girl*.

"Joining Motown was more like being adopted by a big loving family than being hired by a company," writes Otis Williams of the Temptations in his autobiography, *Temptations*.

"In the early days we were a family . . . we had so many good times together. We had picnics, Christmas parties, or we just hung out," said session pianist Earl Van Dyke, one of the numerous architects of the so-called Motown sound.

Martha Reeves, in her autobiography, *Dancing In the Street*, confirms: "Whenever Motown was called 'a family operation,' the reference to family was accurate. [Berry Gordy's] parents, 'Mom' and 'Pops' Gordy, as we lovingly called them, treated us all as their own. . . . They would both dress up and look so distinguished as they appeared at our openings, sending flowers, telegrams, and wishing us luck."

Gordy himself, finally, adds his bit to this "family" business in the foreword of the 1990 *The Motown Album* (the pun on the word "album" is both obvious and telling, as this scrapbook about the history of the record company is meant to suggest a family album of candid photos). Writes Gordy:

> Our loyalty to one another and to our goals was so strong that the only reasonable description of that energy was something beyond business and beyond contracts—it was the sticking together that only happens in families. . . .
>
> Though we did not coin the term ourselves, the "Motown Family" was not a description any of us took lightly. It was how other people described us, because it was the impression we gave other people. It doesn't matter what really accounted for our being perceived as a family, but I can tell you we all believed that we were. We certainly fought and loved like one.

The family myth resonated in two ways for Motown: First, as applied to an ostensibly black family, the Motown myth was particularly pleasing to blacks for whom "family" and "unity" are nearly fetishistic affections and affectations fraught with political and metaphysical meaning generated by a memory (nay, consciousness) of oppression. Nothing so warms the heart of the average African-American than an acknowledgment—philistine and sentimental as the current spate of Afrocentric greeting cards or gripping and compelling as John Wideman's memoirs—of the wondrous necessity of family. It must be remembered that in 1959, the year

Motown started, Lorraine Hansberry's play about black family life, *A Raisin in the Sun,* burst upon the scene. That play, which combines the worst of a Hallmark greeting card with the best of Russian drama, has endured as well as Motown's music. Second, the family myth meant that Berry Gordy was not merely a CEO, a boss, a leader, or even a visionary but that he was a father, an older brother, an uncle, a coach, a teacher, a guardian, an authority figure motivated by something other than making money from his acts. And the acts, of course, became his children, his brothers and sisters, his wards, his companions and not simply his employees.

This intense paternalism (Gordy's favorite phrase to his sometimes distraught and disgruntled artists was, "I'll take care of you") probably helped the company to survive in its early years. The bitterness and anger expressed in interviews and books by some former Motown artists and employees about their treatment at the company has largely been exacerbated or intensified by what some felt was a myth that was nothing more than self-serving hypocrisy. In short, the paternalism of the early years, and the implicit sense of racial uplift and "community"—fostered by the company's own bourgeois-motivated and practically rendered need in a racist society to have an identity of virtue and racial "commitment"—undoubtedly fostered the sense among many that Motown was not a privately owned enterprise which, in fact, it was, but some sort of cooperative venture. For a time, Gordy was able to manipulate brilliantly both his black and his white audiences by having Motown as vaguely a "race company" satisfy certain nationalistic yearnings for blacks while presenting it as an "assimilationist success story" for whites. He balanced, through his family image, the neurotic need of his black audience for uplift and the equally neurotic need for accommodationist outreach for his white audience.

Part of the family myth was established by the inescapable fact that the company was literally family-run: "Fuller, Esther, Anna, Loucye, George, Gwen, and Robert all worked at Motown along with Mother and Pop. You could find a Gordy lurking in practically every department," writes Berry Gordy. "My own family was and is close," writes Smokey Robinson in his autobiography, *Inside My Life,* "but I'd never seen anything like the Gordys—four sisters and four brothers who made it clear to their lovers and spouses and anyone else that their family came first. The Gordys took care of business, but mainly they took care of each other." The myth of family capitalism was important for Motown, despite the fact that Gordy was unable, as it turned out, to pass the company on to his children, because, in the disreputable business of popular music-making, it gave him the imprimatur of something established, linking, as it were, clan and property or, more properly, in this instance, clan and technic. What is surprising, in an age where, as Daniel Bell pointed out, "the old relation between the two institutions of property and family . . . has broken down," is not that the myth of family capitalism eventually petered out for Motown but that it managed to serve the company for as long as it did and is now a permanent part of the company's image. Motown was, ultimately, built as much on the powerful myth of Gordy's own family as on the myth of "family happiness" he projected and nurtured among his employees, and some explanation of the values that shaped this extraordinary family will help us to understand this extraordinary man.

A Usable Black Present

or the Lessons of Booker T. Washington

and Joe Louis

"Now, look here, Ellen," said Mr. Walters. (He called her Ellen, for he had been long intimate with the family.) "If you can't get on without the boy's earning something, why don't you do as white women and men do? Do you ever find them sending their boys out as servants? No; they rather give them a stock of matches, blacking, newspapers, or apples, and start them out to sell them. What is the result? The boy that learns to sell matches soon learns to sell other things; he learns to make bargains; he becomes a small trader, then a merchant, then a millionaire. Did you ever hear of any one who had made a fortune at service?"

—Frank J. Webb's *The Garies and Their Friends* (1857), an early African-American novel

My objections are, to our glorying and being happy in such low employments; for if we are men, we ought to be thankful to the Lord for the past, and for the future. Be looking forward with thankful hearts to higher

attainments than wielding the razor and cleaning boots
and shoes.

—David Walker's *Appeal to the Colored Citizens of the World*

Is it un-American for us to build our own homes, and
schools, hospitals and factories while we are suffering
and being turned away from many of yours? . . .
Is it un-American for us to build up an economic system
among ourselves?

—Elijah Muhammad's *Message to the Blackman in America* (1965)

Since the black bourgeoisie live largely in a world of
make-believe, the masks which they wear to play their
sorry roles conceal the feelings of inferiority and of
insecurity and the frustrations that haunt their inner lives.

—E. Franklin Frazier's *Black Bourgeoisie* (1957)

How To Build A Nation

James Brown's 1974 "Funky President (People It's Bad)"
was, in its way, a more explicitly racial song than earlier
tunes like "King Heroin" (1972) or "Say It Loud—I'm
Black and I'm Proud" (1968). (And in this song, inci-
dentally, "bad" has no hip ironic meaning in black code.
It denotes precisely what it does in the mainstream.)
Perhaps that is why the tune was a hot black radio hit but
did only moderately well on the white pop charts.

"Funky President" harkened back to tunes like "Don't Be A Dropout" (1966), "I Don't Want Nobody To Give Me Nothing (Open the Door, I'll Get It Myself)" (1969), and "Get Up, Get Into It and Get Involved" (1970). All of these message songs could be called black songs of middle-class aspiration, in their own way, songs of working-class origin (and decided working-class appeal) that envisioned a black middle-brow nationalist world of self-reliance, faith in oneself, civic responsibility, and engagement. "Funky President"—the title itself being a satiric oxymoron, made for the occasion of Gerald Ford's becoming president after the Nixon resignation—has the same message except that it is couched, with some degree of soulfully rendered urgency, in the language of blacks owning businesses, controlling their community, saving their money ("like the mob," Brown sings, thus, another Italian connection). The song suggests, as the matter always has been in the African-American cultural vision, that the imminent demise of the black (since the days of slavery the African-American has never seen his situation here except in the most dire and perilous terms of precarious survival) is coupled with how much and how quickly he can adopt certain middle-class habits of morality and ingenuity.

One is struck by how at odds this remedy of rectitude and cunning bourgeois thrift may seem in relation to the desperation of the problem being addressed, just as it may be odd that a message of self-discipline and self-advancement should be so sincerely presented in a music

that was considered by the mainstream, white culture
such an attack on those very bourgeois, Christian values.
E. Franklin Frazier, in his *Black Bourgeoisie* (1957), suggested that black business enterprise as a "social myth has
been one of the main elements in the world of 'make-believe' which the black bourgeoisie has created to compen-
sate for its feeling of inferiority in a white world domi-
nated by business enterprise." A song such as "Funky
President" and a good deal of James Brown's repertoire (a
song like "It's a Man's World" or "It's a Man's, Man's,
Man's World," cut in 1964, certainly suggests that Brown
saw masculinity tied to material achievements and capitalist well-being) counters Frazier's view by proffering,
first, that the black fantasy about black-owned business
was something more than a middle-class make-believe,
that is, a general make-believe of the race, if Brown's popularity as an artist is any indication; and second, that although this view of business may have been a sign of inferiority, it was also a sign of secular or profane aspiration
for a subjugated people that may be as noble in its reach as
it is tragic in some aspects of its unreality or shallowness.
Perhaps this is one of the points that Zora Neale Hurston
was trying to make with Joe Starks and Logan Killicks,
two different types of male aspirants for bourgeois
respectability, in her 1937 novel, *Their Eyes Were
Watching God.* It meant a great deal to his black fans
when James Brown became the first black performer to
buy a Lear Jet, buy radio stations, cut deals with record
companies, control entirely his stage show, and act, fi-

nally, as the complete and magisterial *auteur* of his own business mission as if, as a business property, he had sprung fully from his own imagination. For a people who feel that their history, in part, is and has been a long line of business abuses and humiliations and thefts on the part of whites, Brown's stature as musician/businessman and as conveyor of middle-class ambition is of no small measure. (The complexity of the myth of entrepreneurship and the meaning of business among African- Americans is something that Nelson George, in his provocative and often insightful book, *The Death of Rhythm and Blues,* seems to oversimplify entirely when he suggests that "[the] rejection of [Booker T.] Washington and the rise of the NAACP meant that the drive to assimilation became the dominant item on the black agenda. . . . Only a minority of blacks would openly agitate for more self-sufficiency." The drive to have businesses and to worship money culture—which Du Bois so eloquently warned against in his 1903 classic, *The Souls of Black Folk,* which George seems to have only selectively read—was a blatant attempt, despite its nationalistic pretensions, to assimilate or a proof of having assimilated!)

"Funky President" was clearly a song that one could hardly imagine any white rock or country artist making or white audience consider interesting, as the American Dream of success is contextualized a bit differently for whites. Their assumptions about it and their cynicism over its emptiness tend not to match black assumptions and cynicism but to run parallel to them, as these assumptions and cynicism represent two distinct forms of a common nationalist mythology. This is largely because blacks and whites tend to see the community and the individual in almost oppositional ways: The white sees the individual's empowerment as a safeguard against the community's tyranny; blacks see the community's empowerment as the safeguard of the individual's dignity and fate. For many blacks, the song probably brought an image of the Nation of Islam and Elijah Muhammad's insistent "Do For Self" message, the current avatar of nationalism and self-respect through empire-building at the time the song was made, although such thinking predates the Black Muslims. Indeed, the Muslims were able to generate a certain regard and esteem from the African-American community because it preaches a line that resonates in such a densely emotional way in those quarters. The dream of blacks owning businesses, being liberated through entrepreneurship, is not new. James Brown himself exploited the image of being a successful businessman in the 1960s and 1970s, although like Elijah Muhammad, his commercial kingdom was less than puffed up to be and disappeared fairly quickly. We might understand Berry Gordy and the making of Motown by understanding that the connections between commerce, the virtue of accumulating wealth, and African-American life and culture is deep, intricate, remarkably philistine, and silly, as E. Franklin has suggested, yet remarkably compelling.

Young Man Gordy and
the Making of Americans

When Berry Gordy, Sr.—one of the many black southern immigrants who came north during the Great
Migration of the 1920s—moved his business from a
rented location to his own building on the east side of
Detroit, his wife, Bertha, a schoolteacher, named it the
Booker T. Washington Grocery Store and, thus, paid
tribute not only to one of the most important black leaders of the 20th century but to a set of values and be
liefs, aspirations and morals, that coalesced around
Washington but were expressed far earlier in African-
American history by such disparate 19th century black
leaders and writers as Paul Cuffe, Frederick Douglass,
Richard Allen, James Forten, Martin Delany, William
Wells Brown, and David Walker, each of whom had
entrepreneurial enterprises of varying kinds, from
churches (the major business endeavor in the black community) to newspapers to sail-making to writing.
Interestingly, even the men listed here who were ex-
slaves are not seen in historical hindsight as southerners
but rather as northern black abolitionists. This last is no
insignificant point, as shall be seen in discussing Booker
T. Washington. If there has been a myth of white
American energy and enterprise that is generated by a
history of national expansion, there has been a corre-
sponding mythical urge of black American nationhood

built on the notions of black energy and self-sufficiency, an urge to separation stimulated by the African-Americans' history of segregation and an urge to achievement fueled by America's own preoccupation with success and ambition and blacks' need to disprove their perceived and storied inferiority.

Booker T. Washington, the figurehead and secular institution builder around whom this urge to black nationhood has received its most ironic articulation, was, in some sense, never really a southerner. In his autobiography, *Up From Slavery* (1901), he informs his reader that his models were Mrs. Viola Ruffner and General S. C. Armstrong, both white northerners. His accounts of his labors in a West Virginia salt mine, his supervision of Indian students at Hampton, and his teaching school back in West Virginia give his early life more of a middle-western than a southern flavor. When the Gordys, called their establishment the Booker T. Washington Grocery Store, it was these very qualities, these signatures of bourgeois rectitude—thrift, Yankee ingenuity, hard work, business acumen, ambition, willingness to do humble, menial work—associated with both the North and the West and championed by Washington that were being commemorated. (And as Berry Gordy, Jr. makes clear in his autobiography, *To Be Loved,* his parents worked very hard to inculcate those values in their large brood.) Washington may have preached to blacks over and over to stay in the South, but a book like *Up From Slavery* makes clear that he was warning them against being southerners by habit.

Few families practiced more fervently or more successfully the success ethic of Booker T. Washington than the Gordys. Berry "Pops" Gordy, Sr.'s father, Berry Gordy, was a highly successful businessman and landowner, and a meticulous record keeper in post–Civil War Georgia, and when the father died tragically during a lightning storm, Pops continued in his father's footsteps: "I always had money; I had money all the time," Pop writes, or more properly recites, in his oral autobiography. Indeed, his success—farming, running a produce and meat business—led to his being forced from Georgia because he had too much money for a black man in the South in those days to be able to avoid coming to a bad end at the hands of jealous whites. In Detroit, he worked as a plasterer, a grocer, and eventually as a printer, and he employed his eight children in his enterprises and taught them the Washingtonian virtues of petit bourgeois success. This, of course, set the precedent for having the family work at Motown for son, Berry, Jr. (In his autobiography, Berry, Jr. suggests that he often found his father's passion for hard work an expression of inefficiency, his father also made several bad or disadvantageous business deals, partly because of his mania for work. Gordy gives two vivid, if brief, examples of how he learned the craft of business dealing by watching Jews.)

Surprisingly for a family with such bourgeois aspirations, Berry Gordy, Jr., as an adolescent and young adult, tried to be a professional boxing champion, a pursuit one would normally associate with the scion of a more economically depressed household. But there were two major reasons for Gordy's boxing ambitions: First, Gordy was born in Detroit in 1929 and grew up during the era of Joe Louis, whose family came from Alabama to Detroit roughly four or so years after the Gordys. (Sugar Ray Robinson, the boxing wunderkind, who was born in Detroit in 1921 but grew up in New York, was also an influence as he and Gordy were closer in weight. Robinson's family had migrated from a farm in Georgia.) Louis was more than a boxer, more than a champion athlete; he was the personification of a broad and compelling black triumph, a symbol of black freedom, assertion, and achievement during an age when blacks experienced rigid segregation and were beginning to become restive about their prolonged degradation and disenfranchisement, and during an age when the heavyweight championship was the most coveted title in all of sports. Louis won the championship in 1937 when Gordy was eight and retired in 1949 when Gordy was twenty. Louis was Gordy's first and probably most impressive hero, a homeboy who made impossibly good. As Gordy, Jr. writes about the time of Louis's 1938 victory over Max Schmeling: "I was only eight at the time, but I knew Joe Louis was a hero, a hero of all the people, but he was black like me. I knew what that meant. Even at eight years old I had gotten a taste of the world—the real world—the white world." Second, Gordy grew up during the Depression when a greater number of boys from working-class, petit-bourgeois, and blue-collar backgrounds (Barney Ross, a Jew, whose father was also a merchant, comes to mind right away) went into the sport as it offered far more money for success than other professional sports during a time when even lower middle-class families were strapped. It was moreover the only professional sport where a black might be able to cash in big. Boxing in the 1930s and 1940s was more a sport for working-class boys than it is today when most of its participants are from what is called the underclass.

Gordy was a decent boxer as both an amateur and a professional but he fought in too light a weight classification—bantamweight and, later, a featherweight—to make much money unless he could do something spectacular like Henry Armstrong and win titles in several weight divisions simultaneously. Apparently, Gordy was not *that* good. His ambition to be a champion boxer in a lighter weight division, however, was not completely unrealistic or unreasonable; during his boyhood, Gordy knew that such lighter weight fighters—that is, divisions below middleweight—as Armstrong, Ross, Lou Ambers, Tony Canzoneri, Jimmy McLarin, and Kid Chocolate had made names for themselves and decent amounts of cash. The failed boxing career affected Gordy in two ways: First, because he quit school in the 11th grade to pursue boxing, Gordy never learned to read or write very well (although he did receive his GED while in the service), which meant, in the end, that Gordy became an intuitive intelligence, something that actually stood him in good stead in the game of trying to anticipate and predict hit records. Second, he learned that in any career pursuit the risks one takes must be balanced by the possibilities of the rewards if the risks are successfully negotiated. He discovered in boxing that the risks he endured as a fighter far exceeded the rewards he might enjoy, even if he became a champion. He eventually decided to gamble on music (something he had always been interested in) because the risks seemed more reasonable and the rewards more fulfilling. Gordy describes his departure from boxing in this way: "Then, one hot August day in 1950, a remarkable thing happened. . . . As I sat down on a bench, my eyes fell on two posters on one of the four square pillars that supported the gym's ceiling. . . .

"The top poster announced a Battle of the Bands between Stan Kenton and Duke Ellington for that same night. The one below was advertising a bout between two young fighters. . . .

"I stared at both posters for some time, realizing the fighters could fight once and maybe not fight again for three or four weeks, or months, or never. The bands were doing it every night, city after city, and not getting hurt. I then noticed the fighters were about twenty-three and looked fifty; the band leaders about fifty and looked twenty-three."

The conjunction in Gordy, Jr. of the Washingtonian practices absorbed from his father and the experience of Joe Louis's heroism meant that he could use the example of, arguably, the two most important and influential pre-1950s black leaders: the "realistic" virtues of the petit-bourgeois habits of industry and tenacity espoused by

Washington and the "idealistic" possibility of an extravagant impact on American popular culture at large à la Joe Louis. It must be remembered that both Louis and Washington, despite the "nationalistic" renderings given them by many blacks, were, in essence, crossover heroes; it was Louis who was cheered, even celebrated, by whites for beating white opponents, something that was unthinkable during the reign of the first black heavyweight champion, Jack Johnson (1908–1915). Louis also became one of the major idols of World War II, a first in American popular culture. It was Washington who ate dinner at the White House with Roosevelt (a striking icon, as many of the civil-disobedience confrontations during the civil rights era occurred at eating places), who extolled white hero figures, and who suggested that blacks could, too, adopt the values of white Protestant America. Both the ideas of a usable black male heroism and of a crossover appeal to whites as well as high-class blacks—two models steeped paradoxically in the contrary worlds of straight-laced middle-class respectability and the larger-than-life, street-corner world of masculine derring-do—would have enormous and obvious effect on Gordy, Jr., in creating his vision for Motown. In combining the lessons from Louis and Washington, Gordy, indirectly and inadvertently, learned something from the other major black figure of the century, W.E.B. Du Bois. It was Du Bois in his famous remark about black double-consciousness in his seminal *The Souls of Black Folk* who said:

The history of the American Negro is the history of this strife—this longing to attain self-conscious manhood, to merge his double self into a better and truer self. In this merging he wishes neither of the older selves to be lost. He would not Africanize America, for America has too much to teach the world and Africa. He would not bleach his Negro soul in a flood of white Americanism, for he knows that Negro blood has a message for the world. He simply wishes to make it possible for a man to be both a Negro and an American. . . ."

As Du Bois suggests, a black can be neither just a Negro (that is, exist purely and solely on the basis of his racial consciousness), nor can he be just an American (that is, exist purely and solely on the plane of a national, nonracial, mythic consciousness) without, in either case, losing a vital dimension of his identity. Gordy, from the examples of Washington and Louis, in essence, learned how to merge the identities of being black and being American and this merging was key to the formation and success of Motown. Gordy, with the music he was to create, pinpointed, as did Du Bois, the precise identity neurosis of both blacks and whites: the African-American's fear that he will be bleached into whiteness and the white's fear that he will be Africanized. The one fears the tragedy of being a mulatto, the other the degradation of being a mongrel. Gordy managed to negotiate these neuroses by appealing to American youth through music that neither bleached nor blackened, although, of course, from the margins, throughout his career, he was accused simultaneously of doing both.

After an uneventful if unsatisfying stint in the army (unlike Pops, Gordy, Jr., was unable to contrive an early discharge), Gordy, like most young people in search of themselves and a career, went through a series of jobs during the fifties, but in this case they fortunately prepared him for the career culmination as head of his own recording company. Initially, Gordy worked in the family's print shop or with the family's plastering business, doing back-breaking work in either instance. As Nelson George writes in his book on Motown, *Where Did Our Love Go?*: "Pops wouldn't accept anything less than hard work from his boys. He believed in nepotism, but not as an excuse for inferior workmanship." In 1953, Gordy married Thelma Louise Coleman, and with a loan his father managed for him from the church credit union and his army discharge pay, Gordy started the 3-D Record Mart, a retail store that specialized in jazz records. "I was always a jazz lover," Gordy said later, "I loved Billie Holiday. In terms of other jazz people, I liked the ad-libbing ability, which is really another form of songwriting, of Charlie Parker or Sonny Stitt, Lester Young, Miles Davis, Thelonious Monk, Art Tatum." Gordy, something of a hipster, had been hanging out in the jazz scene in Detroit and thought he could turn his passion into a money-making venture. In two years the store closed because few Detroit blacks wanted to buy records by Charlie Parker and Lester Young, much preferring the leading performers of the Rhythm and Blues craze, Louis Jordan, Johnny Ace, Ivory Joe Hunter, LaVern Baker, and Faye Adams. As saxophonist Johnny Griffin said, the promoters "took [jazz] out of Harlem and put it in Carnegie Hall and downtown in those joints where you've got to be quiet. The black people split and went back to Harlem, back to the rhythm and blues, so they could have a good time." Oversimplified as an explanation, as David H. Rosenthal in his book, *Hard Bop,* asserts, but nonetheless, in broad measure, correct.

After the failure of the record store, Gordy, who had begun working at Ford's Wayne assembly plant and whose marriage was not in good shape (eventually he and his wife separated, but having three children merely intensified the pressure he felt to find some way to make money) began to hang around the fringes of the R and B world, passing himself off as a songwriter. With the help of his sisters, Anna and Gwen, who had secured—in typical Gordy go-getter fashion—the photography and cigarette concessions at the famous Flame Show Bar, Gordy was introduced to several musicians, including Maurice King and Thomas "Beans" Bowles, both of whom would eventually work for Motown (along with pianist Earl Van Dyke, bassist Jimmy Jamerson, and drummer Beeny Benjamin, the rhythm section that would give Motown recordings their unique thrust), managers, hustlers, nightclub owners and other types who populated the subterrestrial world of black American popular music during the age of segregation. In 1957, Gordy, determined to be a full-time songwriter, began writing songs for another Detroit ex-fighter, Jackie Wilson, "Mr. Excitement" as he was called on the chit'ling circuit, who, along with Clyde McPhatter—both of whom came out of Billy Ward and his Dominoes—were among the most renowned R and B voices of their time. "In early 1957 music was literally everywhere," Gordy writes. "Now that music was my business, I wanted to be a part of all of it." Several of Gordy's songs, written for Wilson between 1957 and 1959 in partnership with Tyran Carlo, aka Roguel Billy Davis, became major hits: "Reet Petite" (Gordy's parody of Elvis Presley), "Lonely Teardrops," "To Be Loved," "I'll Be Satisfied," and "That's Why I Love You So." Gordy realized little money from these hits, as royalties for songwriters took a long time to materialize, and in the free-and-easy world of R and B were not likely to be paid completely. Moreover, Gordy did not publish his own tunes at this time, which meant he was at the mercy of the music publisher and the record company Wilson recorded for to give accounts of sales, something he was just not likely to get from them.

In 1958 Gordy met Raynoma Liles, a trained musician with perfect pitch, who was to become his second wife. She encouraged him to produce records—that is, take responsibility for a song's arrangements, harmonies, mixes, and the overall structure and presentation of a record—a move that eventually led to the formation of Hitsville, or Motown Records. Within a year, he had scored a medium hit with Marv Johnson's "Come to

Me" and a major hit with Barrett Strong's "Money (That's What I Want)," the former recorded at the famous Hitsville building on West Grand Boulevard, the latter on his own Tamla label, and had discovered a teenaged group—Smokey Robinson and the Miracles—that could deliver his sound to a young audience. His initial capital came from an $800 loan from the Gordy family kitty, Ber-Berry Co-op. He knew right away that he wanted to run his own company. In 1961, Gwen married Harvey Fuqua, the former lead singer of the Moonglows and the man responsible for bringing Marvin Gaye to Detroit, who resurrected Anna's company through his own, Harvey and Tri-Phi Records, forming Anna-Tri Phi. These companies were soon bought out by Berry Gordy. They provided him with the Spinners, Shorty Long, Junior Walker and the All-Stars, and (probably most important) a singer named Lamont Anthony, who, under the name of Lamont Dozier, became part of the famous Holland, Dozier, and Holland songwriting team at Motown. With the arrival in 1960 of street-wise William "Mickey" Stevenson, the first of a series of "hot," richly creative record producers, the pieces were in place. Motown was born.

Reviewing Gordy's career up to the founding of Motown, it is clear how each of his missteps helped him ultimately. The 3-D Record Mart failed not simply because Gordy was selling the wrong product; he switched his stock to what his patrons were buying, but the store still failed. Somehow, this early on, Gordy had little interest in, or his temperament had little tolerance for, being a petit-bourgeois merchant. He somehow wanted to shape and influence taste and music and not merely supply a product to fulfill a need. He decided to reorient his listening habits and his taste to the new sound of R and B because he realized that this potentially was new cutting-edge music. Presumably, he was regularly reading *Billboard* (virtually every record-store owner did and does), the magazine of charts and trends in the record industry, during his years as a record-store owner, and he certainly would have noted the issue devoted entirely to R and B published on April 24, 1954, or articles such as one entitled "Death Certificate Premature: R and B Ain't Ever Been Sick" in the July 25, 1955, issue. Finally, from the record store, he learned about record distribution and how records can be best marketed for the public and precisely what publics exist for which records.

His job at the Ford plant, as Nelson George and other critics have pointed out, made him aware of two things: how production can be efficiently organized and automated for the highest quality. At Motown during the sixties, producers could also write songs and songwriters could produce, but artists—either singers or session musicians—were not permitted to do either. With this type of control, Motown put out a highly consistent product. It was in the 1970s when the artist became both producer and writer—in short, when the album became a "work" in black music and the artist became an *auteur*—that Motown faltered, as Gordy was uncomfortable with that trend. His disagreements with Stevie Wonder, Marvin Gaye, Diana Ross, and the Jackson 5 over this point are well known. From his auto plant experience, Gordy also became aware that to keep his company going, it was necessary to provide a series of attractive rewards and incentives for hard work, as well as an elaborate system of shaming for laziness. A record company, like an auto company, requires an almost unbearable atmosphere of competition. Gordy believed in competition with the fervor of a fanatic. (This intense sense of contest not only created a celebrity system within the company but became a point of celebration about the company, a virtual mark of internal and external prestige.) Thus, producers with hit records at Motown were given more studio time, and the others had to fight for what was left. The hottest songwriters were allowed to work with the hottest singers. At company meetings, Gordy bluntly criticized any song or performance he considered inferior, not permitting the song to be released, thereby angering his producers and songwriters, but also spurring them to do better in order to curry his favor and approval. This system produced an unprecedented number of hit records in relation to the number of records released. Gordy also learned how the wave of the future was the tinny-sounding car radio, where most young people were first to hear new records. Motown records were always mixed to sound well coming over car radios. Finally, the Ford job taught him that he could not accept anonymous menial work under a stranger's direction. He knew there was absolutely no future in it. As Elliot Liebow perceptively points out in his classic work, *Tally's Corner*: ". . . the busboy or dishwasher who works hard becomes, simply, a hard-working busboy or dishwasher." Or assembly-line worker, in the case of Gordy.

His work as a songwriter introduced him to one essentially creative phase of the production of mass-directed popular music, and from it he learned how songs are put together and how they are recorded. Gordy was musically illiterate; he could neither play an instrument (he can doodle on the piano by ear and play what is called "arranger's chords") nor read music but he had a great sense of what constitutes a good pop-cum–R and B song, as both Raynoma Gordy Singleton and Smokey Robinson testify in their autobiographies. He was—like many others who came into popular music at this time, to use Alec Wilder's pejorative term—an "amateur." What frightens the trained musician is the idea that someone who is an "amateur" can make music successfully simply by understanding music not as an art, nor as a highly complex set of techniques or an elaboration of rules, but rather as a series of effects and gimmicks that can be manipulated by anyone with an ear and some imagination. What angered traditionalists was that the coming of people like Gordy was, in effect, the deconstruction of popular music, the explosion of it as a contrivance and a strategy and not the continued reverence for it as an artistry and a craft. Pop traditionalists feared that Rock and Roll was not merely formula—that was acceptable—but was illusion, a parlor trick that mocked music itself. In an age when many feared the manipulative powers of a burgeoning mass culture apparatus, from C. Wright Mills on the left to Whittaker Chambers on the right, such a response was hardly surprising. Gordy's rules for songs were simple but effective: Always use the present tense; never overdo the hook; make sure the song has a hummable melody, which means that it should be like something the public's heard before; find originality in the song's concept, in how its lyrics are phrased, in its rhythm. Like the young white songwriters and producers who reorganized Tin Pan Alley through overly orchestrated pop–Rhythm and Blues of the late 1950s and the early 1960s at the Brill Building or with what became known as the Brill Building Sound—Berry Mann and Cynthia Weil, Carole King and Gerry Goffin, Doc Pomus and Mort Shuman, and Leiber and Stoller who churned out songs for groups and singers like the Drifters, the Coasters, the Shirelles, Ray Charles, and Ben E. King—Gordy did not write songs, he wrote *records*. The point was for the singer to serve the song, and not the song the singer. It was a common practice, for instance, for producers Mickey Stevenson and Brian Holland to use additional voices in mixing the recordings of the Marvelettes, one of Motown's successful girl groups, to make them sound smoother and fuller. The girls in the group, apparently, never knew this at the time.

Because additional voices, string orchestras, and

other effects were added to many Rock and Roll records, fans were often disappointed when they heard these groups and singers perform in person. Unlike jazz artists whose "live" performances were expected to exceed their recordings, Rock and Roll performers were often a great deal less in person than their records. This is why James Brown's first *Live at the Apollo Theater* album, recorded in 1962, was such an epochal event in the history of Rock and Roll, as it proved, by becoming one of the best-selling R and B albums of that year, that some forms of this music could be captured live with great effect. It remains Brown's biggest-selling album, never yielded a hit single, and reached number two on the pop charts in the summer of 1963. At this time, of course, live recordings in jazz were routine, with most major artists having one or more such recordings to their credit. Motown, with even more daring innovation, scored a big hit in 1963 with a live single of Little Stevie Wonder, "Fingertips, Part 2," modeling the young artist after Ray Charles, who recorded a live album in 1959 that inspired Brown. This song launched Wonder's career. Motown thus helped to further the possibilities that at least some live Rock and Roll could be effectively recorded. Interestingly, these two records succeeded, in part, because they offered, like a jazz record, live instrumental prowess—in Brown's instance, his entire band, one of the best in post–World War II popular-music history, and in Wonder's instance, because of his solo harmonica playing. In effect, both Wonder and Brown were authentic auteurs with these records. Nonetheless, these exceptions only further prove the rule that Rock and Roll records were studio contrivances, and neither songwriters nor producers cared one whit how these performers sounded in person.

Gordy essentially had some of the same aesthetic principles as the Brill Building crowd but his sound lasted longer, was more encompassing—covering soul jazz–cum–R and B with the organ/sax combo of Junior Walker and the All-Stars, to the frantic parody of doo-wop with the Contours, to its reinvention as sophistication by the Temptations through the crossover combination of the Andrews Sisters, the Shirelles, and the Davis Sisters in the Supremes—and made an even bigger impact on the culture at large.

"Most Afro-American's can't sing pop," said James Brown in his autobiography. "They may think they can, but they can't." While this may be true, it is almost equally true that if they cannot sing pop, they can be made to *appear* to sing it. Brown himself did this on such early songs as "Try Me," "Prisoner of Love," and the aforementioned "It's a Man's, Man's, Man's World," for he surely was no pop singer. If Brown's songs make the pop charts, however, then what is pop? Is it merely a technique that can be mimicked by anyone, a set of conventions and gestures that can be adapted by anyone with a sense of what the market likes? Or does pop music have an aesthetic of its own?

Among Motown's singers, only Diana Ross had a truly "pop" voice, that is, an absolutely depthless, completely synthetic voice, but Gordy found ways to make many of his singers seem pop. He changed the late Mary Wells from R and B to pop by making her singing less strident and less rooted in the black gospel tradition. On Wells's first record, "Bye Bye Baby," which she wrote, her voice is hoarse and harsh (partly owing to the number of takes), with intense melismatic flourishes and shouts, the sort of vocal ornamentation that would please a black church audience but might leave many whites indifferent. Once Smokey Robinson began to write for her, however, her style became softer, her voice relaxed and sweet, poignant and cute, and her lyrics adolescent.

Robinson's songwriting was essential to Motown's early success. He had a great ear for love lyrics that were familiar but not clichéd. But what made a great tune, say, out of the Temptations' "My Girl" was the tension between its rather sentimental words and the late David Ruffin's strong gospel-fueled voice, which threatened to break out of the song's pop sensibility at any second. (Ruffin was, along with Levi Stubbs of the Four Tops, Motown's most dramatic male voice.) Gordy, like the Brill producers, encouraged Robinson and his other songwriters to use this contrast. The idea was to give the pop audience a pop tune with a nonpop voice. Holland, Dozier, and Holland did this to great effect with their melodramatic, overwrought songs for the Four Tops.

Yet without a trained musician such as wife Raynoma as a trusted second who shared his vision, Gordy would have had greater difficulty getting the Motown

Sound off the ground. He needed someone who could write lead sheets for the musicians, who could make sure the background singers were performing in the proper harmony, and who could transpose keys if the original key of a song was inappropriate for the singer. But Gordy was not only a man of considerable talent and vision, he was also a person who could spot and exploit talent in someone else. Yet despite what Gordy brought to his own career, without certain historical and technological forces at work, Motown would never have been born.

The technological changes are easy to enumerate: the birth of the transistor, the long-playing album (33⅓ RPM) and the single (45 RPM) in the late 1940s, and the emergence of television as a mass-culture contraption in the 1950s. It is difficult to say whether these changes were the cause or the effect of the explosion of interest in music among the general public but, as Jacques Barzun points out, music had become, by the 1950s, "a passion-ate avocation," a change in attitude that "amounts to a cultural revolution." People grew more intensely inter-ested in music not only once it became an artifact (com-mercial recording started in the 1910s) but also when it became ubiquitous through sound movies, radio, hi-fi, television, and the like, that is, once it became divorced from an actual live performance or occasion and could exist as a representation of itself. Moreover, in the 1950s—the age of the Cold War and intense ideological debates over the fate of the world, as well as intense scrutiny about the nature of political and intellectual commitment demanded from each citizen—music (because for the nonmusician it is nonintellectual, an escape form ideology and ideas) may have been especially attractive at this time, in the same way as becoming the hipster—Mailer's White Negro (many white Los Angeles teens were trying to become cholos as a sign of hipness)—to escape into some romanticized idealization of a racial minority's identity was another means of escape from the Cold War pressure of constricted and constrained identity options.

The effect of the invention of the transistor was similar to the later invention of the microchip: It made electronic appliances smaller and cheaper, particularly radios. In fact, it spurred the growth of portable radios, which had an enormous impact on where music was listened to and on the mating habits of people who used music on the radio for sensual purposes. The LP became the "adult" record of the market and the industry's best-selling format as well, since most recorded music was packaged in this way. (Sinatra, for instance, was the leading seller of LPs in the 1950s, and Columbia Records started their record club in 1955 geared to adults with LPs of pop, easy listening, jazz, and classical.) The 45 single became the format in which Rock and Roll was presented to the public. It was not until the late 1950s—the time of the emergence of Motown—that the 78 RPM was phased out of the R and B market. This was an important event as it signaled that black popular music and white popular music were available in the same format, making crossover easier. Rock and Roll and Rhythm and Blues were largely seen as "singles"—that is, 45 RPM music—it was not until well into the sixties that these forms began to exploit the album format as an artistic concept and not simply as repository of a few hit singles and a bunch of B sides. Finally, television was of major importance in the dissemination of the new youth and black popular musics, largely through such shows as Dick Clark's "American Bandstand," which later spawned "Shindig" and "Hullabaloo"—shows essential to Motown's success, which were simply rebuilt versions of "Your Hit Parade"—and older variety shows like the "Ed Sullivan Show," all of which gave an aura of respectability to black music by making it appear more mainstream.

Television was also the final kiss of death for jazz as a popular music. Because jazz was used so much as background music for TV shows in the 1950s, it became relegated in the public's mind to incidental or programmatic or, worse, mood music that was not meant to be listened to, with hardly a personality of its own. Moreover, for the youth of America and for many blacks, jazz became a kind of staid establishment music as a result of television's cooption and its own self-conscious intellectual pretensions. There were exceptions, such as the popularity of Henry Mancini's theme for the show, "Peter Gunn"; the cool jazz of Miles Davis and the Third Stream of Dave Brubeck and the Modern Jazz Quartet; the midsixties recordings of drummer Chico Hamilton that featured Memphis reedman Charles Lloyd, bassist Al Stinson, and Hungarian guitarist Gabor Szabo, which were considered especially hip among the black cognoscenti; the piano stylings of Ahmad Jamal and Oscar Peterson; and, for the black masses particularly, the growth of organ-sax-guitar soul jazz combos: Jimmy Smith's, Brother Jack McDuff's, and Jimmy McGriff's, or the hard, gospel-tinged bop of Horace Silver and Cannonball Adderley that indicated a consuming preoccupation among blacks with presenting themselves artistically in complex, exaggerated poses as primitives in touch with a more spiritual core while being superb, if intimidating, technicians whose music could not be covered by whites.

In this respect, the two most influential musicians for the African-American masses between 1955 and 1970—the two instrumentalists who were considered most deeply black—may very well have been organist Smith and Texas-born, honking tenor saxophonist and bandleader King Curtis (born Curtis Ousley), who led or participated in sessions at Enjoy, Scepter, Prestige, and Atlantic Records, among others, the last three being among the most important independent companies putting out popular black music during this period, the last specializing in Rhythm and Blues and jazz. Curtis, who was murdered in 1971, became an important purveyor of R and B, funk, soul jazz, and Memphis Soul, all the major areas of popular instrumental black music, from 1950 until his death. (The honking tenor saxes and the screaming Hammond B-3, the latter straight from the black church, never much appealed to whites, who thought the sound to be raucous and loud, with little artistic pretension or principle that made much sense to them. James Brown, however, successfully crossed over this aesthetic in his music, where his vocal style and band arrangements approximated the screams and honks of this style of jazz. In fact, in his autobiography, Brown said that he disliked the blues and saw his music as a form of jazz.) But generally jazz was being pushed off the scene as a popular force of the magnitude that it had been in the past.

The historical forces that helped make Motown possible are a bit more complex in their rendering. But one particular historical happening seems very clear: Just as Frank Sinatra saw the 1960 election of Kennedy as something portentous, as a signification of a new era (because, as many have said, he felt that he was delivering a president to his friend, Chicago mob chief Sam Giancana, who purportedly produced the 200,000 Chicago votes that provided the margin of victory), so too, for vastly different reasons, did Gordy. As Raynoma Gordy writes in her *Berry, Me, and Motown*:

> To Berry and to me, President John Fitzgerald Kennedy symbolized the idealism we shared—the belief that doors would open for us, that anything was possible. . . . It was an awe-inspiring time. JFK was new and

fresh, young and exciting. So was his wife. And *we* [Berry and I] were all those things. I'd look at their picture in the paper and think how romantic they were. Like us.

At no time in their history did blacks feel more optimistic about the future than in 1960 when things were changing, when a young president's rhetoric was promising so much and so richly, when a young black southern preacher was speaking so eloquently for a brave new humankind, and it was quite possible, at last, to think of entering the world of whites without going through the back door of the culture.

The Midwest as Musical

Mecca and the Rise of

Rhythm and Blues

Detroit was a real music town. You heard it everywhere, from radios and record players, outside the doors of the clubs that kids like us were too young to enter legally, from guys and girls standing out on the street singing. It sounds like a scene out of a musical, but that's truly how it was.

—Otis Williams, *Temptations*

Nowhere else in the nation and at no other time have blues musicians ever been more firmly dedicated to the proposition that it don't mean a thing if it ain't got that swing than in Kansas City in the early 1930s.

—Albert Murray, *Stomping the Blues*

It was in Chicago that "King Porter Stomp" was first recorded, by King Oliver in 1924. It was in Chicago that it was made popular by Benny Goodman, playing a Fletcher Henderson arrangement of it in 1936. And of course it had been in Chicago that black musicians had gathered together to share talent and ideas during the

Columbian Exposition of 1893—this looked forward to
Chicago's Century of Progress Fair of 1933, after which
that city became the most fertile ground for jazz, later
called "swing." Jazz was not of course conceived in
Chicago, but it was most certainly incubated there.

—Dempsey Travis, *An Autobiography of Black Jazz*

Writers both in and outside the region agreed that the
Middle West had replaced the East as the standard by
which to gauge other sections of the nation.

—James Shortridge on the heyday of the Middle West as
idealized American region in his *The Middle West: Its
Meaning in American Culture*

White and Black Middle West

"That's my Middle West," wrote F. Scott Fitzgerald
through the voice of narrator Nick Carraway toward the
end of his 1925 novel, *The Great Gatsby,* "not the wheat
or the prairies or the lost Swede towns, but the thrilling
returning trains of my youth, and the street lamps and
the sleigh bells in the frosty dark and the shadows of
holly wreaths thrown by lighted windows on the snow. I
am part of that, a little solemn with the feel of those long
winters, a little complacent from growing up in the
Carraway house in a city where dwellings are still called
through decades by a family's name."

But the snow and the houses of the middle-western

city struck Richard Wright's protagonist, Bigger Thomas, differently in the seminal 1940 novel, *Native Son*:

> As the car lurched over the snow [Bigger] lifted his eyes and saw black people upon the snow-covered sidewalks. Those people had feelings of fear and shame like his. Many a time he had stood on street corners with them and talked of white people as long sleek cars zoomed past. To Bigger and his kind white people were not really people; they were a sort of great natural force, like a stormy sky looming overhead, or like a deep swirling river stretching suddenly at one's feet in the dark. . . .
>
> After a few feet [Bigger] stopped and swung the light. He saw dusty walls, walls almost like those of the Dalton home. The doorways were wider than those of any house in which he had ever lived. Some rich white folks lived here once, he thought. Rich white folks. That was the way most houses on the South Side were, ornate, old, stinking; homes once of rich white people, now inhabited by Negroes or standing dark and empty with yawning black windows.

Fitzgerald, a white native midwesterner who came of age as a writer during a decade when several other midwesterners—Sinclair Lewis, Glenway Wescott, Theodore Dreiser (who started before the others), and Sherwood Anderson—were examining midwestern life, might be expected to have a different view than Wright, a black native southerner, who came north to flee the intense segregation and racism of the South, only to be thwarted and embittered by the North's own version of segregation and racism. Even in earlier novels, such as Langston Hughes's *Not Without Laughter* (1930) or Jean Toomer's *Cane* (1924), where the Middle West is prominently featured as either big city or small town, in one case by a native midwesterner and in the other by a borderline southerner from Washington, D.C., it is perceived differently—not nearly so idyllically as Fitzgerald's, yet unambiguously better or at least decidedly different from the landscape of the Deep South. Even in some of the works of a more contemporary writer like Toni Morrison, *Sula* (1974) and *Song of Solomon* (1977), this is clearly true.

It is notable that blacks have always referred to the area of Kansas, Nebraska, and Oklahoma as "the territory," a designation implying both space, escape, and freedom that they never applied to any place in the South or along the northern Atlantic seaboard. As Alain Locke reminds us in his 1925 essay, "The New Negro," black southerners did not go to the North and West spurred simply by necessity but by the same hope for advancement and economic opportunity that moved Europeans to come to America in the late 19th century and earlier. (Interestingly, the premiere of "Amos 'N' Andy" on radio in 1925, destined to become the longest-running and most popular show in radio history, showcased for the first time in American popular culture, on a regular basis, a black community—albeit, created by two white men—in this instance, in Chicago, the heart of the Middle West.) That all did not turn out as African-Americans would have liked does not diminish the fact that in the Middle West, blacks experienced greater freedom personally in many instances and clearly saw greater freedom among the whites (part of the mythic history of the Midwest is the value placed there on egalitarianism) than they witnessed in the South, and this, undeniably, had an indelible effect on their national character, so to speak. The myth of the Middle West as the symbol of American pastoralism and the center of American urban industry influenced how blacks who came from the South saw the country and themselves. As James Shortridge suggests in his *The Middle West: Its Meaning in American Culture*, ". . . the Middle West is defined essentially by its relationship to the West." In effect, coming to the Middle West meant that blacks confronted the mythology of frontier, wilderness, and urban design, the various cultural ways that Americans go about the business of thinking about nature and spaces, in a much different formulation than in the South. (The Middle West came into vogue as a significant regional term in 1912, just as its myth as an American place was being fully and triumphantly articulated, a mere few years before the beginning of the great black migration from the South. So, we have an interesting conjunction of a place defining itself at the same historical moment as a people are beginning to redefine themselves.) In his autobiography, *Miles,* Miles Davis made much of his Illinois roots when he compared his outlook to that of fellow jazz trumpeters Dizzy Gillespie and Louis Armstrong: ". . . I'm from the Midwest, while both of them are from the South. So we look at white people a little differently." He elaborated when speaking of saxophonists Charlie Parker and Coleman Hawkins: "We—Bird, me and Bean—were all from the Midwest. I think that had a lot to do with us hitting it off musically and sometimes—at least with Bird—socially; we kind of thought and saw things alike."

Ralph Ellison explains the significance of his midwestern background in the introduction to his collection of essays, *Shadow and Act* (1964):

> Anything and everything was to be found in the chaos of Oklahoma; thus the concept of the Renaissance Man has lurked long within the shadow of my past, and I shared it with at least a half dozen of my Negro friends. . . .
>
> One thing is certain, ours was a chaotic community, still characterized by frontier attitudes and by that strange mixture of the naïve and sophisticated, the benign and malignant, which makes the American past so puzzling and its present so confusing; that mixture which often affords the minds of the young who grow up in the far provinces such wide and unstructured latitude, and which encourages the individual's imagination—up to the moment "reality" closes in upon him—to range widely and, sometimes, even to soar.

What Ellison suggests here and throughout *Shadow and Act* when he discusses his Midwest is that it was in "the territory" that African-Americans, perhaps for the first time, certainly with more intensity than they had had before, learned something about living in a democratic culture, limited though it may have been, which led to the fantastically humane and harshly disciplined development of their music. They learned how to feel truly what they were instead of how they should feel or pretend to feel for whites. It was as if life in the slave quarters had finally been given space to expand and air to breathe.

Midwestern Swing

One of the best black swing bands—one of the best swing bands, period—was based at Detroit's Greystone Ballroom from 1926 through 1941, although its glory years were roughly from 1928 to 1934. The Greystone was probably "owned" by the Jewish-dominated Purple Gang, which controlled graft and bootleg booze in Prohibition-era Detroit, a key city in smuggling foreign liquor because of its proximity to the Canadian border. And the new hot black music called jazz, as the early careers of Cab Calloway, Duke Ellington, and Earl Hines can attest, became the central feature of the ambience of gangster-controlled nightclubs, to the patrons entertained and drinking. Led by circus drummer William

McKinney and star trumpeter and arranger John Nesbitt, McKinney's Cotton Pickers (Jean Goldkette's booking agency gave the band its condescending name) became a particularly redoubtable band when the famed Don Redman became musical director in 1927, leaving Fletcher Henderson for whom he had written scores from 1923 to 1926. The band had the propulsive drive of, say, Count Basie or Jay McShann and immaculate ensemble playing of, say, Jimmy Lunceford or Fletcher Henderson. Along with the Savoy Sultans of Swing, McKinney's Cotton Pickers were probably the best unsung swing band in jazz. They built their reputation almost entirely in the Midwest.

It is one of the least recognized facts of American popular culture that the Middle West—an area that runs from, say, Cincinnati to Kansas City, from Detroit to Oklahoma City, from Chicago to St. Louis, from Alton, Illinois, to Little Rock, Arkansas—is responsible for most black popular music in America. From Scott Joplin to Miles Davis, from Charlie Parker to Jimmy Rushing, from Curtis Mayfield to Sam Cooke, from Jimmy Blanton to Donny Hathaway, from the Isley Brothers to Brother Joe May, the Gospel Thunderbolt of the Midwest, this area was pivotal in the development of virtually every style of black music. The Middle West is where jazz came in the 1920s when King Oliver and Louis Armstrong migrated to Chicago. It is where blues became a formalized 12-bar musical pattern at the turn of the century, in places like St. Louis and Evanston, and where it became electric with the coming of the great post–World War II bluesmen like Muddy Waters, Howling Wolf, Buddy Guy, Elmore James, B. B. King, and Little Walter. It is where jazz redeveloped and redefined itself as swing in Kansas City in the 1930s and it is where Charlie Parker emerged from the Jay McShann band to reshape jazz as bebop in the 1940s. Illinois native Miles Davis made jazz cool in the 1950s, and Missourian Chuck Berry reinvented Rhythm and Blues as a youth music that a white deejay from Cleveland, Alan Freed, was to call Rock and Roll. From Coleman Hawkins to Screamin' Jay Hawkins, from Joe Turner to Tina Turner, from Milt Jackson to Michael Jackson, from Roland Kirk to Bobby Watson, the Middle West has been a central, even mythological, location for black popular culture and black popular music. And the three principal musical cities in this area have been Detroit, Chicago, and Kansas City.

From Detroit alone, after World War II, came such talents as Yusef Lateef, Thad, Hank, and Elvin Jones, Della Reese, Little Willie John, Tommy Flanagan, Kenny Burrell, Jackie Wilson, Barry Harris, Donald Byrd, Aretha Franklin, Paul Chambers, Roland Hanna, Alice Coltrane, and Charles McPherson, as well as, of course, the talent that came out of Motown after 1959. Why did Detroit become such a hothouse of musical talent after the war? It is difficult to pinpoint a precise answer but part of it lies in the intense emphasis on musical education among Detroit blacks. It is a common myth that blacks learn about music in their churches and like all myths it has a considerable amount of truth. Yet black secular music education provides as much, if not more, training for blacks who seek a music career than churches do. For instance, Ralph Ellison, in writing about jazz guitarist Charlie Christian, describes music education in the black Oklahoma school he attended: ". . . harmony was taught from the ninth through the twelfth grades; there was an extensive and compulsory music-appreciation program, and . . . a concert band and orchestra and several vocal organizations."

At the turn of the century, E. Azalia Hackley, a light-skinned black woman from Detroit who was trained as a soprano, adopted the musical education of black youth as her mission; she was called "Our National Voice Teacher" in the black press and was wont to stop for 15 minutes during her recitals and give her audiences lessons in musical appreciation and voice training. From Hackley's instructorship to that of such storied black Detroit public-school music teachers as Ernest Rodgers, Orville Lawrence, and James Tatum, Detroit black youth have been reared in a vibrant musical atmosphere in their public schools. The annual E. Azalia Hackley Program featuring black composers and black classical performers started in 1943, and such noted black Detroit performers as Rogie Clark, Robert A. Harris, and Charles Coleman (also music critic for Detroit's black newspaper, the *Michigan Chronicle*) have been featured in various years. Indeed, an aspect of black music education that is not as written about as it should be is how much blacks, in their schools, are exposed to classical European music, marching-band music, and pseudo-classical show tunes, and how much these forms of music have been traditionally enjoyed in the black community and not necessarily by the black bourgeoisie only. Blacks have often found some of these forms as attractive, as much a part of their cultural language—as they rightly should—as the musical forms that are more expressive of their own African-derived aesthetics and sensibilities, and this has influenced overall the shaping of their popular music.

Consider this fact about Motown: The three major early groups of the company—the Supremes, the Temptations, and the Miracles—were put together and rehearsed at their high schools. They were not church groups; in fact, the members did not attend the same church, and in various autobiographies there is little talk about the influence of the black church in their music. For instance, Smokey Robinson speaks about the influence of Sarah Vaughn, and Mary Wilson singles out the McGuire sisters, Doris Day, and Patti Page as her personal favorites when she was growing up (an indication, among other things, that the popular-culture broadcasting devices—radio and television—not only exposed white audiences to black music but, just as important, exposed black audiences to white music, and that black musical taste could be just as pedestrian as the white mainstream or that white mainstream tastes ought not to be routinely stereotyped and dismissed more so than black tastes are subject to be). Black music has been equally a product of secular and sacred forces and impulses. One finds this is true equally of Ray Charles, who became closely tied with the secularization of black gospel although he never learned his craft in a black church but rather at the school for the blind he attended and on gigs, and of Michael Jackson who, true to his Motown roots, also put a great deal of gospel fervor into his music but who had "music class and band in the Gary [Indiana] schools" where he grew up.

Here are two undeniable facts: First, Motown could not have happened without a strong public-school music-education program in Detroit, even if many of its performers were musically illiterate. The session musicians, the arrangers, and often the producers were not, and nearly all of them were trained in the public schools of Detroit. Moreover, the performers themselves received some musical training and exposure to music in school, which in many instances turned out to be highly influential. Second, Motown could not have happened anywhere else but in the Middle West, despite the fact that the greatest number of R and B independent labels were located in Los Angeles. (This is not where the greatest number of black artists originated or honed their craft, and as blacks were mostly shut out of both the movie industry and Las Vegas during the Cold War period of 1945 through 1960, Los Angeles was not an especially supportive environment in many respects.) For it was in the Middle West, finally, until 1970, despite New York doo-wop and the Brill Building, Philadelphia with the Twist, the Italian teen idols, and Kenny Gamble's record store at 15th and South Streets, or the proliferation of record labels in Los Angeles and a bopping Central Avenue down South Central Way, where the creative crucible of black music existed.

Crossing Over

But Motown would not have succeeded without a crossover rise in the interest in black music, particularly in postwar Rhythm and Blues. Several factors conjoined to make this possible: First, after the war, big bands and swing were passé, particularly because big bands were no longer economically feasible. Ellington and Basie, veritable institutions and the most important big bands in American music history, continued to produce new and exciting music, but most black bands disappeared, and those white swing bands that continued, with the exceptions of Stan Kenton, Buddy Rich, and Woody Herman, became, in effect, fossilized "oldie" acts.

Second, the invention and growing popularity of the electric bass changed entirely how popular music was conceived; contemporary popular dance music eventually was built around the sonic phenomenon of the electric bass. Electric instruments generally tended to find their first practitioners among black musicians because they were usually regarded in white mainstream circles as being freakish, novelty items. After blacks have created a system of playing these instruments the better to reinvent their own music, white musicians will then begin to use them extensively and create further innovations.

Third, the popularity of white covers of black Rhythm and Blues in the 1950s conferred a kind of respectability and mystique on the black versions, which led many white teenagers to seek out the real thing in curiosity and in quest of hipness (as was shown in Alan Freed's *Mister Rock and Roll,* for instance). These same white teenagers helped fuel the entire youth culture movement and many of them wound up figuring in the civil rights movement, in part because of their exposure to this music. Teens, with more expendable money, became a real presence in the mass marketplace in the 1950s. What made Motown possible was not that Elvis Presley covered R and B but that Fats Domino, in the end a more significant artist, not only crossed over with R and B hits in 1955 but with a Country and Western tune, "Blue-berry Hill."

What was indeed far more radical than the Presley success in the mid- and late-1950s was the prominence of three black male romantic balladeers and show-tune singers—Johnny Mathis, Nat King Cole, and Sammy Davis, Jr., by the end of the decade. Davis made it big in the 1956 Broadway show *Mr. Wonderful,* which was specifically written for him by Jule Styne. Cole, enjoying many years of crossover success since 1948 with "Nature

Boy" and "Mona Lisa," had a short-lived television variety show in 1956 (although the show was unable to find a single national sponsor). By then he had become one of the most successful ballad singers in American popular-music history. Mathis broke big with "Wonderful, Wonderful," in 1958, made an album of standard romantic ballads in 1959 entitled *Open Fire, Two Guitars,* and became not simply a successful singer but, with youthful good looks and slick hair making him appear, to white and black taste, a bit exotic like an Indian, he was, in short order, a teenage heartthrob among both black and white girls. He appeared on his album covers more in idealized and stylized drawings and photographs than virtually any other black male artist of the period. Indeed, in *Life Magazine*'s 1958 feature on Rock and Roll, whose "most numerous fans are girls aged 8 to 16"—an article, in effect, about teen idols—Johnny Mathis is the only black singer mentioned, and with an accompanying photograph, especially surprising as Mathis's singing style was not remotely Rock and Roll.

Black male singers found it difficult to make it in romantic balladry because of the open sexual appeal needed for the music to go over with women listeners. The entire white commercial music establishment frowned upon, and felt great unease about, making a black male a legitimate sex symbol. Indeed, the fear of miscegenated sex appeal explains, in part, why such true black Rock and Roll artists as Chuck Berry, Fats Domino, or Little Richard were not promoted as were lesser white teen idols. The other factor was age, as many black male artists associated with Rock and Roll, like Berry and Domino, were considerably older than the white girls who were crazy about their records. But the success of Mathis, Cole, and Davis—which came about in part because the black male as sex symbol was making his presence felt in popular culture in the 1950s—was an enormous breakthrough that helped ease the way for Motown artists, although the first genuine black male Rock and Roll teen idol would be Twist King Chubby Checker, who did not record for Motown. (Interestingly, Checker, in an emergency for Dick Clark's "American Bandstand" show, covered R and B performer Hank Ballard's "The Twist" for a huge crossover hit in 1960, the first time a black crossed over by covering a black R and B tune, creating a dance craze in the process. Checker's youth and manner, and his lack of reputation as an aggressively sexual R and B artist, put the song over for white mainstream audiences, including adults. Gordy had never been a fan of Ballard's more salacious material, such as the mid-1950s hits, "Work with Me, Annie" and "Annie Had a Baby," and with his unerring sense for cultural trends, starting with the comic book industry's self-imposed, self-regulatory code of 1954 to rid itself of exposed breasts and horrific violence in the name of protecting America's youth, he made sure that in crossing over, Motown's music never brought with it R and B's more debauched element of good-timing jungle bunnies in the ghetto.)

The fourth factor that made crossover possible was the breakup of the music entertainment industry, caused by the decline of big bands and of the power of the Hollywood film in the 1950s due to the growth of television. New York Tin Pan Alley composers no longer reigned supreme. The major record labels—Columbia, RCA Victor, and Decca (soon to be MCA)—were being challenged by trend-setting small independent labels. Most R and B was recorded for small independent labels, as was a good deal of early Rock and Roll, bebop and soul jazz. Specialty in Los Angeles, King/Federal in Cincinnati, National and Atlantic Records, both in New York, Sun Records in Memphis, Apollo Records in New York, Chess Records in Chicago, Modern Records and Imperial Records in Los Angeles, and Savoy Records of Newark, New Jersey, are just a few of the companies that proliferated like mushrooms in the dark seeking local black music after World War II. As Arnold Shaw pointed out near the end of his book, *The Rocking 50s,* a comparison of the top pop songs of 1939 and 1959 found that in 1939, the Top Ten pop discs were made by only three companies—all located in New York—whereas in 1959, 39 companies produced Top Ten records and these were located in ten states. Popular music in America was truly becoming regionalized and more open. Moreover, the music that was most likely to attract adventuresome kids, the music that the majors had white artists covering, was the music of the small independent label.

By the time Gordy started Motown in 1959, he was

not thinking, as many indies owners were, that having a white cover of their own R and B was the ultimate mark of success. Gordy was thinking not only that the Motown publishing catalogue would be covered—which it has been much to Gordy's fabulous enrichment—but that Motown recordings would stand up as pop hits on their own, without benefit of covers, which has turned out to be true as well. This is how Motown changed American culture: by Gordy's insistence that *his* performers be able to sell the company's songs to whites and that *his* performers be able to play at the better-playing white venues. Gordy's objective always was to reconfigure what was meant by pop music, to reiterate in his approach that pop was as black as it was white. In this regard, perhaps the most remarkable album the Supremes made was the 1967 issue *The Supremes Sing Holland, Dozier, Holland,* wherein the group sang the songs of their producers, who happened to be, at that time, the hottest songwriting team in America. A black pop group legitimated the music of a black pop writing team and HDH's songs legitimated the Supremes. Nothing quite like this had ever happened in American popular culture before. (Ella Fitzgerald's 1957 *Duke Ellington Songbook* comes close.) And to emphasize the point, four months later Motown released the next Supremes album: *The Supremes Sing Rodgers and Hart.* They had been authenticated as a significant interpretative and stylistic group of singers, and HDH was on par with the great songwriters of Tin Pan Alley and the American musical theater.

Regarding Gordy's vision of reshaping and exploding the racial underpinnings of pop music, he took advantage of his time and place: From the early 1960s fascination with folk music, to the mid- and late-1960s quest to acknowledge the sources of popular music in urban electric blues and early forms of 1950s doo-wop, R and B, and rockabilly, there was a search for authentication and authenticity in pop music despite (or perhaps because of) its contrivance and its falsity—the sheer artistic and emotional vacuity of much of it. This "authenticity" is a service that blacks have learned to provide for American popular culture, though what was really being authenticated was the separation of black music as "race records," which was largely a political act to keep black music (and black artistic expression, generally) understood popularly as a marginal phenomenon. Motown changed this with its huge success, moving black music, largely on its own terms, within the popular-music mainstream, negotiating, with considerable aplomb, the enterprise of authenticating itself as youth music, while acknowledging, even celebrating, the R and B sources of African-American music, reaffirming, in an astonishing cultural wave, the innovative power of R and B as a pop music. The deep complexity of the quest for authentication in popular music lies in the extraordinary happenstance that all cultural innovations are subject to cooptation by a mainstream that tends to "normalize" or nonspecialize the innovations for mass consumption. These societal instances of reenforcing marginality while thwarting it by erasing its existence as a threat produces, ultimately, in differing ways, among both the elites and the masses, an urge for more authentication and innovation. This is the elementary dynamic of creation in a capitalist culture. Within a little more than a decade, from 1945 to 1959, from, say, Louis Jordan to Ray Charles, the first wash of "authentic" black music, R and B, began beneath bourgeois moral (this is dirty music), political (this music promotes race mixing and disturbs the status quo) and commercial pressures (this independent music is undercutting the power of the major record companies) to experience its own dilution and decadence, moving from a marginalized but artistically rigorous avant-gardism into an orthodoxy of mediocrity. That, as much as anything, made possible the success of Motown (and to a lesser degree its rivals Atlantic and Stax) in the 1960s era of renewed authentication, and the quest for authentication was made all the more vigorous because black people—with a revitalized political consciousness and momentous political agenda that for the first time in American history had a huge impact on the culture at large—desired it so very much.

In the 1960s the only other force in black American popular music that rivaled Motown as an authenticator was James Brown, the Godfather of Soul himself. As Bruce Tucker, coauthor of Brown's autobiography, points out, Brown was not a product of Stax, Atlantic, or Motown, but a sort of freelance presence in black music in the 1960s; and after 1965, when he became a pioneer in funk—or a kind of extremely rhythm-based, almost antisong, rifflike dance tune, he began to undermine Motown's "crossover" influence through new groups like Sly and the Family Stone and through his influence on a wide variety of established black artists, including Miles Davis, Jimi Hendrix (during his Band of Gypsies phase), Herbie Hancock, and Motown's own producer Norman Whitfield, who all began to formulate tunes in the studio based on musicians playing counterriffs on an improvised bass riff. In other words, in the late 1960s, and certainly by the early 1970s, during the height of the black power and black pride movement, many younger blacks thought Motown sounded too "white," too crossover, and not authentically "black" enough, but this was not actually a realization that grew from Motown's "sound" as much as from its marketing success and the growing tendency for young whites to co-opt Motown as their own cultural authentication. Young blacks felt simply that this music "cannot authenticate them and us, too and still be our music," as one black collegian told me back in 1972. Interestingly, Hendrix, Davis (in his electric phase from 1970 to 1975), and Sly Stone—mentioned above as three artists influenced by the funk innovations of Brown—were also influenced by the pop crossover innovation of Motown, and each had a large crossover audience. And each, in his distinct way, became entangled in the limitations of both funk and crossover, in ways that both Brown and Motown avoided, becoming in the end hideously costumed minstrels unable to escape the cultural entrapment of black "rhythm" as a stigma of stereotyped black male sexuality and clownish showmanship that became an artistic cul-de-sac. (Black life and music in America has been sullied by its two most striking characteristics: rhythm and fervor, two musical and psychic features that whites have convinced themselves that they intrinsically lack, so much the better that they might have a neurotic need for the Negroes in their midst who supply them in abundance! Motown and Brown built their music on both rhythm and fervor, but Motown managed to transcend them so that both became in Gordy's vision assertions of Negro soul and adumbrations of the American pulse of creative "force," while Brown monopolized them as blatant individual expressions of American entrepreneurial energy and drive. For both Motown and Brown, rhythm and fervor became new versions of multiplicity, of the dynamo.) That all three men—Davis, Hendrix, and Stone—in different ways, despite their remarkable success commercially and artistically, were destroyed by drugs by the mid-1970s was not surprising, even, in some ways, predictable.

Gordy could imagine that his own R and B indie would become a pop force because of the success of black-owned Vee Jay Records, located in Chicago. (There had been other black-owned record companies including, for instance, W. C. Handy's Black Swan Records, started in 1921, and Excelsior Records, launched in either the early 1930s or early 1940s, depending on one's source, by Leon and Otis Rene from Louisiana.) Started in Gary, Indiana, in 1953 by Vivian Carter and James C. Bracken, along with Vivian's brother Clarence who became the company's top A and R man, Vee Jay grew to be one of the most successful indies and one of the most successful black businesses in American history. "The company had a phenomenal track record," said Randy Wood, who became president of the company in 1963, "usually producing a hit with an artist's first or second release." The company started by recording black gospel because such acts were cheap and plentiful around Chicago but soon expanded. Among the artists Vee Jay had in its stable by 1961 were Jimmy Reed ("Ain't That Loving You, Baby," "Honest I Do," "Baby What You Want Me to Do"), Dee Clark ("Raindrops," "Hey, Little Girl"), Jerry Butler and the Impressions ("For Your Precious Love"), the Dells ("Oh, What a Nite"), the Spaniels ("Goodnight, Sweetheart, Good-night"), and the El Dorados ("At My Front Door"). They were to have eventually the Four Seasons ("Sherry," "Walk Like a Man," "Big Girls Don't Cry"), Betty Everett ("It's in His Kiss or The Shoop Shoop Song"), the Beatles ("Do You Want To Know a Secret?" "Please Please Me," "From Me to You," "Love Me Do," "Twist and Shout"), and Gene Chandler ("Duke of Earl," "Rainbow"). Vee Jay also had a number of successful jazz acts in their catalogue, including several sidemen from Miles Davis's mid-1950s quintet: Wynton Kelly, Paul Chambers, Philly Joe Jones, and

Cannonball Adderley, as well as Wayne Shorter, who would join Davis's band in the 1960s, and Lee Morgan. Indeed, the company was generally more successful at promoting white acts and pushing non–R and B and non–pop material than Motown—most of whose excursions into something non–R and B or non-pop, such as the Melody label (Country and Western), Black Forum (spoken word, political activist), Rare Earth (white rock), and Workshop Jazz, were all aborted without sustained success. But Vee Jay also understood well its black R and B audience and their spending and listening habits. "The ghetto communities—black, Mexican, and Puerto Rican (and Mexicans and Puerto Ricans are heavy into black music as well)," Randy Wood notes, "spend proportionately more money on records than do whites. One cat will call up a friend, 'I've got the new Aretha album,' and the other will say, 'I've got Issac Hayes,' and suddenly they get a party together that way. Black music is really an integral part of the way blacks live."

Nonetheless, by 1966 when Motown was attaining the height of its glory, Vee Jay Records was going bankrupt, largely through management shake-ups and intense internal bickering between its black and white executives and among the blacks themselves. (One reason that Gordy exercised such strong control over Motown, always approving all of its product and never placing the company's stock on the market for public sale when he hit the big time, was probably to prevent internecine conflicts that could have destroyed the company.) Ewart

Abner, Vee Jay's top executive whose departure badly hurt the company, was, it is said, like Berry Gordy for whom he would eventually wind up working, an inveterate gambler as well as notorious for keeping accounts in his head. (Abner was and is incredibly knowledgeable about black popular music and how it is put together in a recording studio and has been a considerable asset to Motown.) Gordy, then and possibly still a gambler, was known for having lost considerable sums at Las Vegas and other high-rolling tables. It was, in fact, rumors of Gordy's gambling losses that sparked the commonly held belief that Motown was taken over by organized crime in the mid-1960s. It is impossible to say whether this is true; virtually everyone connected with Motown past and present, including Gordy himself, denies it. Nelson George, in *Where Did Our Love Go?*, makes a persuasive argument against it. In any case, there is a certain capacity for huge risk-taking among some pop-record executives. As Robert Pruter writes in *Chicago Soul*, "To be an executive in an independent record company, which depends on a continued production of hit records for its month-by-month existence, is to be a naturally gambling type."

Vee Jay was also hurt, though not irreparably, by the damaging loss of its two top white acts—the Four Seasons and the Beatles—to major labels, which may have intensified the squabbling between the white and black executives about the direction of the company. But from Vee Jay Gordy learned that it was possible to run a black-owned record company that could have crossover appeal, that could get its records played on white radio stations and pushed in white record stores. Vee Jay acts such as Jimmy Reed and John Lee Hooker sold very well in white markets. This vision not to restrict himself to just a black market was largely responsible for Motown's success, in contrast to the gun-toting Don Robey who started Peacock Records—another important black-owned indie—in Houston in 1949 and built an extraordinary blues, R and B, and gospel catalogue, including Johnny Ace, Bobby Bland, the Dixie Hummingbirds, "Gatemouth" Brown, Big Mama Thornton, the Mighty Clouds of Joy, and the Caravans.

Gordy could imagine the possibility of not restricting himself to just the black market because the period in which he shaped his vision through his apprenticeship in music—the 1950s—was the age of cultural crossover for the African-American in some striking, symbolic ways: Gwendolyn Brooks was awarded the 1950 Pulitzer Prize for poetry for her collection, *Annie Allen*. Ralph Ellison won the National Book Award for his 1952 novel, *Invisible Man*. William Demby in his 1950 novel *Beetlecreek* and Richard Wright in his 1953 novel *The Outsider* both explored existentialism and modernistic despair and dread as major themes instead of social protest. James Baldwin established himself in the 1950s as the most popular black American writer of his day; his essays appeared regularly in the most respected high-brow and middle-brow magazines, and his books were beginning to appear on the best-seller lists by the mid-fifties. Between 1945 and 1956, Baldwin, Chester Himes, Zora Neale Hurston, Richard Wright, and Willard Motley were among the black writers who wrote novels that featured white characters exclusively. Sidney Poitier became a major Hollywood film star, playing dignified if pressured characters, a far distance from Stepin Fetchit, Willie Best, Louise Beavers, and Mantan Moreland in the 1930s and 1940s; he opened the decade playing a doctor trying to make it in a white hospital against accusations of incompetence in *No Way Out,* played Africans three times during the fifties in *Cry, the Beloved Country* (1952), *Mark of the Hawk* (1955), and *Something of Value* (1957), and ended the decade in *Porgy and Bess* as Porgy (a role he did not want) and as Walter Lee Younger in *A Raisin in the Sun,* both stage play and film. Lorraine Hansberry's 1959 *A Raisin in the Sun,* the most famous of all black plays, posed both the African and the American, the nationalist and the assimilationist, perspectives of the black national mentality when, on the one hand, Beneatha—who adopts the natural hairstyle or Afro as it was to be called a decade later—considers marrying the Nigerian, Agasai, and when, on the other, Walter endorses his mother's decision to move to a house in a white neighborhood after he confronts the white "welcoming committee" of Mr. Lindner who wants to buy him out. In effect, the play suggests that the African-American will be saved only through his acceptance of the three strands of his history: as a proud African who had civilizations and nations (Beneatha's halting love of Agasai), as the inheritor of the patience, endurance, dignity, and love characterized by the females of his family (Lena and Ruth), and as a proud American who came from, as Walter acknowledges, generations of obscure laborers (Walter Lee and his father).

The age of the cultural crossover encompassed much more than the literary and cinematic, however; Jackie Robinson, with obvious rage and sublime restraint, integrated Major League Baseball in 1947 and won the Rookie of the Year Award, one year after the Supreme Court outlawed racially restrictive housing covenants and five years before the Supreme Court outlawed "separate but equal" public school systems. Floyd Patterson—Catholic, intensely assimilationist, Olympic champion in 1952, ambiguous about his profession, clearly a different kind of personality from Joe Louis—became the youngest heavyweight boxing champion in history when he defeated Archie Moore for the vacant title in 1956. By the 1950s, the Negro crossing over to the mainstream had become—through Jackie Robinson—an heroic national icon and—by Supreme Court decree—national public policy.

On the other hand, crossing over meant for many blacks a new kind of activism, a keen sense of nationalistic community embedded, in an ironic yet typically American way, in the idea of integration not through simple if noble endurance of degradation but through a persistent acknowledgment of claims—from court cases like *Shelley v. Kramer* in 1948, to the Brown decisions (ruling and implementation) in 1954, to marches in the street, to the resurgence of Pan-Africanism. In this respect, the 1950s was the coming of age, the maturity of the black bourgeois consciousness as an urge to change and, paradoxically, to challenge the white racist mind, purify the American democratic vision. In short, the 1950s taught us that there could be no democratic consciousness without a realization of the black and, further, that there could be no democratic impulse without a recognition of black consciousness as an essential mode in the national character. This is what Ellison's *Invisible Man* was all about, and although it rejected black nationalism in the form of the antique character, Ras, the book vehemently endorses the idea of community among black folk and, even more meaningfully, in depictions such as Trueblood's family, the Golden Day, and a politically active Harlem—*the recognition of the significance of what that community wants and what it is to the overall meaning and structure of American culture.* Ellison may have thought that black folk in America were unquestionably American, and not African or primitive epigones to serve either a neurotic black or white imagination, but he did not, for a second, think that being American meant being white. James Baldwin, in his collection of essays, *Notes of a Native Son,* published in 1955 and easily the most impressive of his 1950s' books, reiterates Ellison's assertions. In this series of essays, Baldwin creates critical and aesthetic space for himself by denouncing the social protest mission for the black American writer. And he rejects his father's religion and secular vision of life, and, finally, any attempt to be anything other than both American *and* black, both "a bastard of the west" and a citizen of a world that "is white no longer, and [that] will never be white again." Baldwin also articulated memorably the complexity of what ties black and white together, something that Berry Gordy could not have expressed as well but intuitively understood: "It must be remembered that the oppressed and the oppressor are bound together within the same society; they accept the same criteria, they share the same beliefs, they both alike depend on the same reality." But the maturation of this intricate consciousness created not simply a black market to be served by black businesses or a black community ennobled by its own quest for self-definition, although these two are, doubtless, important, but rather what was brought forth was a complex black public that demanded to be served and recognized by the larger society itself. The election of the Rev. Adam Clayton Powell, Jr., to Congress in 1945 and what he articulated through his rhetoric and behavior while there is very much a symbolic rendering of the black, R and B "nation," in effect, as a triptych: a market that demanded public accommodations, goods and service, and equal value and access for its dollar with the whites; a community worthy of respect for its accomplishments and acknowledgment of its aspirations; and a public that sought a reflection of its own varieties of tastes and types in the larger world.

If America entered the Cold War as the strongest, richest, and freest nation ever in human history (some would question the last, of course), blacks, despite their constrained circumstances, had to fill a certain bold expansiveness and a tempered sense of responsibility as citizens, inadvertent or not, of this republic. Jackie Robinson's response to Paul Robeson in 1949 when summoned before the House Un-American Activities Committee seems more fraught with complexities than perhaps might appear at first blush. Robeson had said that blacks would not and should not fight in a war against the Soviet Union: "We do not want to die in vain anymore on foreign battlefields for Wall Street and the greedy supporters of domestic fascism. If we must die, let it be in Mississippi or Georgia. Let it be wherever we are lynched and deprived of our rights as human beings. Let this be a final answer to the warmongers. Let them know that we will not help to enslave our brothers and sisters, and eventually ourselves." Robinson, obviously the most famous college-educated black person in America at this time, was called especially by Congress to refute what was, to many whites, a statement tantamount to treason. Part of Robinson's statement read:

> White people must realize that the more a Negro hates Communism because it opposes democracy, the more

he is going to hate any other influence that kills off democracy in this country—racial discrimination in the army, segregation on trains and buses, job discrimination because of religious beliefs.

If a Communist denounces injustice in the American courts, or police brutality, or lynching, that doesn't change the truth. . . . A lot of people try to pretend that the issue [of discrimination] is a creation of Communist imaginations. . . . But Negroes were stirred up long before there was a Communist party and they'll stay stirred up long after the party had disappeared.

The fact that Robinson and Robeson had different points of view that were of national concern and were articulated and presented in the national media is, of itself, of considerable significance. Robinson wants very much to disentangle black protest from leftist causes and Marxist identification (something that both Richard Wright and Ralph Ellison—leading black intellectuals of the period who, during the 1930s, had been "fellow travelers"—would do in the next few years with their literary works), because it devalues the nature of the protest in the eyes of whites, making them think, as many did at this time, that blacks were not even capable of realizing, on their own, the degradation of their position, and that the only whites who could possibly be interested in black people's affairs, their culture, their company, would be communists (mostly Jews, who, according to white mainstream thinking, are, to a great extent, responsible for the liberalism and atheism of the

modern world) and extreme left-wing whites. It was important to the assimilationist position of someone like
Robinson to emphasize the reality and persistence of discrimination, but to give the lie to the idea that the races
could not and have not come together in America except
under a radical European political philosophy that endorses totalitarianism. Robeson, on the other hand, takes
the leftist view of a "colored world" (after all, to many
Europeans, Russia itself, which Robeson professed to
love, was an Asiatic nation) that must throw off
European and white American imperialism, fueled by
capitalist greed and unbridled racism, that keeps the
darker nations under foot for economic convenience and
white aggrandizement, in order to achieve self-determi-
nation and, through this, a truly just world. In his view,
how can the United States preach freedom and democracy to the colonized "colored" world while maintaining
its own rigid racial caste system?

In this regard, the most important book by an
African-American written between 1945 and 1960 was
W.E.B. Du Bois's *Color and Democracy: Colonies and
Peace,* published in 1945. For in this volume, Du Bois—
who was to be as harassed in the 1950s as Robeson and
ultimately left the United States to live in Ghana—was
to articulate the theory of a "colored" global faction
where "[c]olonies are the slums of the world . . . the
places of greatest concentration of poverty, disease, and
ignorance . . . centers of helplessness, of discouragement
of initiative, of forced labor, and of legal suppression of

all activities or thoughts which the master country fears or dislikes." In short, the colonies resemble African-American ghettoes. Democracy is destroyed by racism and the forces that wish to keep down the people of color in the world. Thus, "[t]he Negro problem forces the United States to abdicate its natural leadership of democracy in the world and to acquiesce in a domination of organized wealth which exceeds anything elsewhere in the world." As the "colored" world, in its fight against European and Euro-American domination, began increasingly to associate nationalism with racial consciousness, so the African-American, through the racism he experienced in the United States, began to reinvigorate his thinking about belonging to a larger black world, about blackness being transnational, of belonging to a Diaspora, if only because American racism, as Du Bois pointed out, forced him to do so:

> . . . in the Immigration and Naturalization Service of the United States Department of Justice passengers arriving on aircraft are to be labeled according to "race," and race is determined by the stock from which aliens spring and the language they speak, and to some degree nationality. But "Negroes" apparently can belong to no nation: "Cuban," for instance, refers to the Cuban people "but not Cubans who are Negroes"; "West Indians" refers to the people of the West Indies "except Cubans or Negroes"; "Spanish American" refers to people of Central and South America and of Spanish descent; but "Negro" refers to the "black

African whether from Cuba, the West Indies, North or South America, Europe or Africa," and moreover, "any alien with admixture of blood of the African (black) should be classified under this heading" ["Negro"].

It is, thus, no insignificant fact that as some members of the black elite began to reinvent, in effect, the reinvention of an "African" consciousness for black people in the 1950s—something that continues to this day, and something that black folk have been doing in this country since the 18th century—Motown, in its own middle-brow black aspirations, became the first record company to open an office in Africa. Du Bois's book sharpened and intensified the views of someone like Robeson, but they were not necessarily views that Robinson would have found absolutely incompatible with his own. Robinson, after leaving baseball at the end of the 1956 season, became a staunch advocate of black business building, conservative Republican politics, integration, and civil rights marches.

The fact that the black public was split about the exchange between Robeson and Robinson revealed that both views had adherents and held weight among African-Americans. Robinson, who specifically mentioned discrimination in the armed forces before the Congressional subcommittee because he had been acutely and intensely affected by it, knew, as undoubtedly did Robeson, the story that during the war Lena Horne had made a stop for the black USO to entertain black troops and found them Jim-Crowed, with German prisoners of war sitting in the front. Only in America could the National League's Most Valuable Player of 1949, Robinson, play in a city, New York, and not be able to eat at one of its most famous restaurants and nightclubs, the Copacabana. Only in America could we have such an effort to recognize one's merit and thwart one's humanity coexisting so easily. The Supremes, in the summer of 1965, the summer of the Watts riot, became Gordy's first act, the only all-girl group, the first R and B's group, and the first black pop act, to play the Copa, an extraordinary breakthrough in the annals of American popular culture. By 1965, the Supremes could eat there, too.

In 1955, the "colored" nations of Asia and Africa, the world faction that Robeson and Du Bois spoke about, met in Bandung, Indonesia, to consider their role in a world where European colonialism was now being challenged. The conference of so-called nonaligned or Third World nations became the figure and model for African-American unity, of African-American nationalism that Malcolm X, former street hustler turned Muslim, used in one of his most famous speeches, the "Message to the Grassroots," given in November 1963 in Detroit alongside one of that city's most popular bourgeois black Christian preachers, Albert Cleage. It was Cleage who was to become the radical race-conscious counterpart to Detroit's most famous black preacher of the day, the Rev. C.L. Franklin, father of Aretha Franklin, and considered by some to be something of a rogue and an Uncle Tom, despite his undeniable brilliance in the pulpit. (Sun-Ra's "ultra" band music of the 1950s also conjured up the vision of a "colored universe.")

And in 1955 Rosa Parks refused to give up her seat to a white man on a bus in Montgomery, Alabama, just a few months after Emmet Till, a Chicago boy, was lynched in Mississippi for whistling at a white woman or asking her for a date. In both events—one an affirmation through assertion and the other a furious denial through a falsely proclaimed innocence—we have America cringing at confronting the reality that simply will not hide itself anymore: the reality of a miscegenated culture where, beneath the mask of an inhuman racial etiquette where everyone supposedly was as separated as the twin beds in the bedroom of nearly every 1950s TV sitcom, in this mannerly ill-mannered age that was to give us the completely unruly sixties, there lurked the unquenchable thirst of interracial sex, which is, finally, what the "new" popular music as (aural, oral, and visual) spectacle in the 1950s relentlessly pantomimed, a false separation that only revealed the culture's essential fusion all the more tellingly and inescapably. Motown was the most grand and most mythic version of this spectacle, this American moment of entrapment between debasement and heroism, between art and cheap commercialism, between infantilism and something suggesting a kind of disciplined liberation, between the best and the worst of both the democratic impulse and black consciousness.

In October 1962 the first Motown Revue left Detroit on a ten-week tour, with the Marvelettes, Marvin Gaye, the Supremes, the Contours, and others. The bus tour took them through the South and the Midwest during the height of the civil disobedience phase of the civil rights movement. In May 1961 the first freedom riders had left Washington D.C. on Trailways and Greyhound buses en route to New Orleans in an attempt to desegregate terminal rest rooms and eating facilities. The freedom riders were beaten, nearly killed, and jailed. The Motown Revue, with so many young blacks on board that it must have resembled a Freedom Tour to some white Southerners, was not greeted quite so harshly; but the Motown bus was shot at, and segregated facilities and uncivil treatment were common. In 1964, when Motown released Martha and the Vandellas' "Dancing in the Street," urban riots were becoming the sine qua non of black frustration. Few blacks accepted the song on its face, insisting that it was a metaphorical theme song for black unity and black revolution. To Motown and Martha Reeves, of course, it was just another dance song. But the music and the history could not fail to conjoin. So maybe it wasn't. Could anyone truly believe that *that* song could come from *that* company, sung by those young black bewigged women, at *that* moment in American history, and not mean everything that all those black folk looting stores and throwing bottles at the police—and making in their rage the unlivable place they lived more unlivable—thought it meant? Yet the young artists knew their significance, as Mary Wilson, one of the bewigged Sup-remes, wrote: "Our tours made breakthroughs and helped weaken racial barriers. When it came to music, segregation didn't mean a thing in some of those towns, and if it did, black and white fans would ignore the local customs to attend the shows. To see crowds that were integrated—sometimes for the first time in a community—made me realize that Motown truly was the sound of young America."

The Shrine

and the Seer

I'd like to hear five recordings of Louis Armstrong
playing and singing "What Did I Do To Be So Black and
Blue?"—all at the same time. Sometimes now I listen to
Louis while I have my favorite dessert of vanilla ice cream
and sloe gin. I pour the red liquid over the white mound,
watching it glisten and the vapor rising as Louis bends
that military instrument into a beam of lyrical sound.

—Ralph Ellison's *Invisible Man*

The deep-rooted Scriptural image of marital union
representing God's reconciliation with his redeemed
people and with the land, the city of Jerusalem, and the
holy temple helped to justify the hotly disputed inclusion
of the Song of Songs in both the Jewish and Christian
biblical canon, by pointing the way to interpret its songs
of sexual passion and union as an allegory signifying the
love and marriage of the Lord to Israel, or of Christus to
Ecclesia, or any of a large number of alternative
relationships. . . . [T]he canonizing of Canticles, with its
candid, detailed, and erotica physicalism, opened up a
rich stock of sensuous imagery on which later writers
could draw to embellish the austerely abstract marital
symbolism of the other books of the Bible. The result of

these complex developments is the paradox that
Christianity, which under the powerful influence of
Pauline theology has been mainly ascetic in its doctrines
and attitudes, has often employed sexual union as its
central symbol for the crucial events of Biblical history,
and for several of the churchly sacraments as well.

—M.H. Abrams's *Natural Supernaturalism*

The Sound of Young America

Red, white, black, and blue(s), Ellison's figurative colors
of miscegenated America (sloe gin, vanilla ice cream,
and Louis Armstrong singing "What Did I Do To Be So
Black and Blue?") are also the figurative colors of
Hitsville, U.S.A. made intelligible through their motto,
"The Sound of Young America"—of the Motown
Museum, now located in the same two buildings on
West Grand Boulevard where it all started. The idea that
Young America, as it were—that is, the America that has
overthrown its bondage to parents and ancestors as models, its filiopietistic homage to black oppression—would
have a "sound," not a voice, is startling yet fitting. As
Jacques Barzun theorized, the public mania for music in
the 20th century is a sign of "an increasing resistance to
words." And a "sound" suggests something that is not a
voice, something beyond and before a voice and thus beyond and before words, something both pre- and post-

civilized. But also suggested by the word "sound" is the African-American slang term for a game of ritual insulting (also called "playing the dozens" but in the Philadelphia neighborhood in which I grew up was called "sounding," each insult being called a "sound"). In that respect, "The Sound of Young America" becomes something subversive and perverse, a cannily contrived insult at mainstream America, cloaked as a seemingly innocent diversion. Here is clearly sloganized the miscegenated vision: the "Sound" being black, and "Young America" being white, as Gordy may have meant it to be, or that black kids could be mainstreamed as teenagers, too. Perhaps Motown, for the first time in American history, gave black kids a mythicized puberty of normal teenage angst.

Black Radio, Black Talk

[I first encountered Berry Gordy] playing music, and I had taken a few of his records. When you do something everybody knows about it. They'd know when I break a record. When I'd go in there and break a record everybody knew that I was doing it. That's how I got to know him. Because I played his music, and made him a lot of money. . . . [My relationship with Berry Gordy] started when [Gordy] started his record company. He had a company but it was very small. He had basically Smokey Robinson. But he had some records out, and he

wanted me to introduce Stevie Wonder and all the acts.
He knew what I was doing here. So he would let me get
the entertainers here first, and if a record came out he'd
get it to me first. As a result people would listen to me,
because they knew I would always have the top records,
and I'd have the Motown Revue when it came through,
and it would have all the stars. He was a very loyal

person. . . .

—James G. Spady, *Georgie Woods: I'm Only a Man,*
biographical account of one of Philadelphia's most
influential black deejays.

Cheerio, My deario
World and cheer-o-et
Cheerio, My deario
There's a tune in the old boy yet
Pip, pip, all that sort of rot
Tally-ho, there he goes,
I'll see you, little darling
And good morning, someone.

—sign-off of Little Lord Fauntleroy, popular black
Philadelphia deejay of the 1950s and 1960s.

But without voices, in this instance the black personality
deejays spinning the platters and their jive, Berry Gordy
would never have succeeded in seducing America with
the Motown sound. (This is a phenomenon distinct
from the white disc jockey of the post–World War period who played Rhythm and Blues on a white radio sta-
tion, in particular Alan Freed, who went on to promote
both Rhythm and Blues and Rock and Roll in a series of

stage shows and cheap but important movies such as *Mister Rock and Roll, Go, Johnny, Go,* which heavily promoted Chuck Berry, giving him a speaking part of considerable presence, and *Rock, Rock, Rock.*) Frantic Eddie Durham of WCHB in Detroit was one of the most important on-the-air pushers of Motown records in the early 1960s. Ken Bell, an important black deejay in the mid-1960s with KJLB in Detroit, says: "If it were not for the black disc jockeys, there would have been no Motown. At first, we broke the records before the white stations did. If a record is not played on the radio, nobody accepts the record. You can't even give it away, if it's not played on the radio. And the black disc jockeys helped Motown get its sound across to the white stations. The black disc jockeys were very, very instrumental and Berry knew this and treated us accordingly."

The importance of the black disc jockey in selling black music predates the coming of Motown. As Nelson George writes: "The relationship between recorded music and radio would be crucial for the evolution of rhythm & blues, since it was to be the first major American musical style to emerge through the playing of its records on the air. . . . Coinciding with the emergence of a vast number of indie labels was the growth of black radio." Gordy, naturally, would have recognized both of these trends during his period as a record-store owner. Radio helped not only to formulate and structure black taste and aesthetics but also to formalize a black market of consumers who could be delivered to sponsors, a black public of listeners who wanted to be informed about matters of importance to them or who simply wanted access to the new medium in order to feel equal to other Americans, and a black community unified by its voices (deejays) and its music, and who could see the radio as a kind of community bulletin board, advice column, and dating service. And black radio provided all those needs.

Bell goes on to discuss the importance of the "black voice" within the black community:

> We had to play the image of being somebody in the black community. We had to be clean and sharp whenever we made an appearance anywhere. A white d.j. could show up in a tee-shirt and jeans but the blacks were highly regarded people in the black community and we had an image to live up to.
>
> Personalities d.j.s are dead now. Taping and the way records are played now killed the market for the personality deejay. Nonstop, 50-minutes of music killed the personality deejay. People are interested in music and not talk. But people still like to hear the d.j.s talk. In the 1960s and the 1970s we were the rappers. People came out to see me at clubs as if I were an artist. Now we have rap music, which shows that people still need to hear talk, still need a voice.

The many men and a few women who became personality deejays on black radio in the 1960s were the voices for the sound, were the voices for the social phenomenon of urban blackness.

Living in the City

Hitsville and Motown as names conjure up both the small town and the big city (Mo' Town?, as a colleague suggested) and, in some way, encapsulate the range of black urban expressiveness and black urban mythology that is the magic kingdom of the metropolis in black American consciousness or, more precisely, in black American fantasy. For, as mentioned above, blacks came to the major cities, to middle-western cities like Detroit, with great hope as European immigrants came to America. One enters Hitsville, the Motown Museum, and is struck by how small it is; it is truly nothing more than a boxlike residential home, oddly enough on a thoroughfare in Detroit where, only a few blocks removed, are the Fisher Building, the General Motors buildings, and the Henry Ford Hospital. But the smallness of Hitsville emphasizes the myth of the black family in two ways: Again, we are reminded by the intimate residential nature of the building that Motown was indeed a "family," and second, we are reminded by its smallness about the small, cramped quarters blacks lived in when they first came to cities like Detroit. And within Hitsville, we find the original recording equipment that was used to make all those hits and realize that the machine—the dynamo, to use Henry Adams's terms—was always a sign of hope and a signification of liberation for blacks, from the car and the machines that produced them, which because of labor shortages beckoned for black hands to operate them, to such machines as the camera, television, and radio which, however waywardly, spread the image of blackness across the land. As songwriter/producer Sylvia Moy said, "We all got excited about that equipment over there [at Motown] and we were able to express ourselves creatively through a lot of equipment that was in that place over there on West Grand."

It may be true, as sociologists Stuart and Elizabeth Ewen state, that "[c]onsumption is a social relationship, the dominant relationship in our society—one that makes it harder and harder for people to hold together, to create community." But Motown as a mode of both consumption and production, indeed, as a stylization—a discipline forged from art and politics—of both, probably held blacks together better than virtually anything else in the black national community, other than the demand for equal rights. That is what the words "Hitsville" and "Motown" signify, finally: a modern black urban community built on technology, on the American bourgeois principles of consumption and production, and on the Washingtonian principles of casting down one's buckets where one is. It was, for a time, an ideal and idealized union of local black organization with a national black sense of mission and destiny.

The Women at Motown

Within the walls of Hitsville one can, through the photos and clippings, the plaques and the album covers, piece together the history of the place. One is appropriately surprised to discover the number of people who have recorded something under contract to Motown: Ahmad Jamal, Sammy Davis, Jr., Tony Martin, Pat Boone, Amiri Baraka, Stanley Crouch, Langston Hughes, Clarence Major, the Last Poets, Rick James, Willie Hutch, the Isley Brothers, Jose Feliciano, Albert Finney, Lynda Carter, Grover Washington, Jr., Teena Marie, and Bonnie Pointer. George Clinton of Parliament-Funkadelic fame was once a staff songwriter for Motown, and Wallace Terry recorded portions of his book *Bloods,* about black soldiers in Vietnam, for the company. And the company continued to be a major force in the 1970s with such artists as Diana Ross, Stevie Wonder, and Marvin Gaye coming into their own and such new major acts as the Commodores (from which Lionel Richie sprang), the Jackson Five, and Thelma Houston. But the company was nowhere like the major force it was in the 1960s when, single-handedly, it staved off the twin invasions of British popular music (from the Beatles, the Rolling Stones, and other groups in Rock and Roll and from Anthony Newley in the theater). From the producer/songwriter era of Smokey Robinson and Mickey Stevenson in the early sixties to Holland, Dozier, and Holland, who wrote and produced most of the Supremes' hits in the mid-sixties to Norman Whitfield and Barrett Strong and Simpson and Ashford at the end of the sixties, Motown enjoyed an era of near dominance in American popular music.

There are, of course, the stories of such other producers and songwriters as Ivy Joe Hunter, Hank Cosby—and Sylvia Moy who rescued the career of Stevie Wonder with the tune "Uptight" when Motown was ready to drop him because his voice had changed. Moy was never given producer's credit for that tune or any other tunes she produced for Wonder at Motown. "I cried, and cried, and cried about that when they weren't going to list me as Stevie's producer," she said. "It nearly broke my heart." Motown was a man's world and no women were ever given credit for producing records. "At that time [1964, when she joined Motown], women did not produce, even though I had the talent and I was producing," Moy continued. "I went to producers' meetings. I was given assignments. I just wasn't given the label credits. I still had my royalties. At that time, women just did not produce. I guess that was just one of those things."

But women were essential to the success of Motown: Raynoma Gordy as musician, singer, publicist, and song arranger; and Maxine Powell, who gave up her own successful charm school and modeling business to tour with Motown acts between 1964 and 1970, and who taught the singers how to walk, talk, hold a microphone, and generally provide the acts with that polished, groomed, and polite presence that made it possible for them to cross over. Although all artists, black or white, need training of this sort to succeed as professional performers, it is especially important for blacks who, as James Baldwin noted, must appeal to mainstream white taste by always being mannerly and likable. (As Beatle George Harrison said on first meeting the Supremes, "We expected soulful, hip girls. We couldn't believe that three black girls from Detroit could be so square!" Whatever stereotype of the urban black street girl Harrison may have been expecting, he was not prepared for a face-to-face confrontation with a fierce black bourgeois ambition that sought to consolidate, not rebel. Martha Reeves describes a similar incident when she and her Vandellas were mistaken for "party girls" by actor Robert Mitchum.) Moreover, this training made the Motown acts more appealing to many blacks because the performers represented a middle-brow impulse to respectability without abandoning their sense of origin. There was also Loucye Gordy, whose extraordinary bookkeeping and bill-collecting abilities kept Motown fiscally sound in the early years when record distributors were slow in paying, tours were not very profitable, and cash flow was tight.

Finally, there was Diana Ross, upon whose back Motown's crossover movement was built once Mary Wells, the singer Gordy originally intended to use to pitch his crossover appeal, flew the coop on her twenty-first birthday after she had several number-one hit records. (She was never heard from again as a major hit-making singer.) Gordy intended from the beginning, to cross over with a woman because he felt that black women were less threatening and, in some ways, more comforting to the white public than a black man would be, especially with the intense sexuality and sensuality that the "new" popular music of Rhythm and Blues and Rock and Roll suggested. The fate of Diana Ross and the Supremes reveals how Gordy saw women as both necessary and expendable. The messy ouster and subsequent pathetic downfall of Florence Ballard—founder of the group and at one time its lead singer until Gordy decreed that Ross has a more sellable and commercial voice—was as inevitable as the unfolding fate in a Greek tragedy. Gordy had no choice but to get rid of one of the women in the group once Ross was made the star in order to show the public and Ross herself that the other women were expendable; the founder of the group was as good as anyone for that symbolic chore. Moreover, it was necessary for Ross's own success that not only Ballard not succeed once she left the group but that the group itself, once Ross left, not succeed. The success of the entire group, once Ross was a star, had to hinge on Ross's presence. Thus, no other woman leaving the group could succeed and the group could not succeed without Ross. (The Supremes, without Ross, had a few successful records, notably "Up the Ladder to the Roof" but quickly faded as a viable act.) In order to make one woman indispensable in the public's mind, several other talented women had to be, in effect, wasted. Not only the other women in the Supremes but the other women singers at Motown, all of whose careers faltered once the big push to make Ross a star started: Kim Weston,

Martha Reeves, the Marvelettes, Freda Payne, Gladys Knight, and Brenda Holloway, to name a few.

When Gordy financed the film *Lady Sings the Blues* (1972) as a star vehicle for Ross, he insisted on so distorting the life of the famed jazz singer Billie Holiday, upon whose autobiography the film is supposedly based, that in effect he simply swallows the life of Holiday into an ocean of pop-culture kitsch for the benefit of Ross. Put another way, what interested Gordy most about the life of Holiday as a vehicle for Ross was precisely what interested Ross herself: that Holiday was the only sufficiently gigantic black bitch-goddess of popular culture whose art could legitimate Ross's own standing as the reigning black bitch-goddess of her own day. Holiday's life, the conventions in black popular music she represented, and the entire reason for her addiction to heroin (abusive men who mistreated her; lack of proper recognition of the magnitude of her artistry) were made expendable for a film bio in the Hollywood tradition of whitewashed garbage. In this film, directed by Sidney J. Furie but orchestrated by Motown's chief executive, Gordy cleverly combined different strands of his crossover appeal element, making Holiday's stint with the white Artie Shaw band (called Reg Henley in the film) the major tour and the only recognizable swing band performance in the film—in effect, making Holiday a crossover star which, in partial truth, she was, although in a far more profound way than the film suggests—while having Ross's Holiday introduced to drugs by one of the whites in the band (bi-ographically untrue), a kind of racist sop to blacks. Ross was nominated for an Academy Award in what had to be one of the worst acting jobs of all time, a combination of gestures that resembled imitations of both Mary Pickford and an hysterical woman victimized by bad psychoanalysis (although this performance is no worse than those of some whites who have won the Oscar).

But the whitewashing of the life of Holiday also ap-pealed to blacks who want, as much as anyone, to have their fantasy lives fit the Hollywood formula of true love and family happiness. Gordy certainly wanted no part of earlier films about black male jazz artists, such as *Sweet Love, Bitter,* made in 1967, and loosely based on the life of Charlie Parker (adapted from the novel *Night Song* by John A. Williams), that starred comedian Dick Gregory, or *A Man Called Adam,* also 1967, starring Sammy Davis, Jr., as a tragic, ill-tempered trumpeter (loosely based on Miles Davis as a model, I suppose, inasmuch as Cicely Tyson, who was Miles Davis's girlfriend at the time, was featured as the love interest in the film) strug-gling for his manhood and his artistic vision in a racist and philistine society. Both of these films end with the deaths of the artists; *Lady Sings the Blues* ends with Holiday triumphant at Carnegie Hall. Gordy's film is not so much about the downfall of a brilliant artist as it is about the struggle of a black woman to become a re-spectable lady in this society with the help of a decent, proud man (an interpretation of Holiday that would have an especial appeal to blacks with a middle-brow impulse). Gordy may have been interested in making Ross a "black Barbra Streisand" but he was just as interested in making both Ross and her male lead, Billy Dee Williams, black versions of, say, Clark Gable and Lana Turner or better still, Clark Gable and Doris Day. In effect, Gordy was interested in creating, for the black public, black stars who transcend the immediate film that the audience may be watching.

He succeeded much better, a year later, with *Mahogany,* which he directed and financed, although the film was not as well received critically and did not do so well at the box office. *Mahogany* is a brilliant film, mythifying, in concise symbolic terms, the middle-brow black struggle for identity. Ross, whose acting is much better here because the role is much closer to her own experience, plays a ghetto-dwelling, struggling, department-store clerk who wishes to be a high-fashion designer. She is accidentally discovered by a famous fashion photographer, played by Anthony Perkins, who makes her into a successful model. In the meanwhile, she is torn between her love for Billy Dee Williams's character, a committed activist in the ghetto running for public office, and her love of success and the artsy European life to which she has grown accustomed. Gordy here has superbly conflated the old Hollywood formula of a woman torn between her career and her man with the identity struggle of the successful middle-class black (Have I left my people? Have I sold out? Do I truly prefer white to black?). There is the usual homophobic distress here in the confrontation between Perkins, whose character is gay, and Williams, whose manhood is never questioned, much to the pleasure of his black audience, as well as the usual conflation of homosexuality, pointless existence, brutal capitalism, inhuman artifice, captive sexuality, and bigotry that characterize Europe and white life, generally, as a kind of velvet chamber of horrors and oddities. Mahogany ultimately returns to the ghetto to help her man, and, thus, returns to her blackness and her people. The film does more to mythify Ross herself as dramatizing the dilemma of crossover success than it does anything else. (Toni Morrison used the same dilemma to good effect in her 1981 novel *Tarbaby,* whose Jadine character is an obvious reworking of both Mahogany and Ross.) In the scenes in the Chicago ghetto, the film does not dramatize poverty or the profundity of that experience as much as it simply does what Williams's character accuses Perkins's character of doing: photographing it for aesthetic contrast and effect. But, naturally, Gordy is not interested in the poor. He is interested in dramatizing only the blacks who wish to succeed, even those who wish to succeed by helping the poor. Gordy proved himself to be an adequate director—competent, in fact—although the film has at times the feeling of a record being slapped together or mixed down. However, he never directed another.

The Shrine

Gordy moved Motown to California in 1970 (it became official in 1972), a move he felt was necessitated by the company's overwhelming success in the 1960s and the importance of expanding in the same lucrative arenas of mass entertainment—original Broadway cast albums, Hollywood films and soundtrack albums, television production—as the major labels in the music business, all of whom are tied to larger mass-entertainment conglomerates. That there is bitterness in the black community because of Gordy's departure, that there is a sense of abandonment and devastation, cannot be gainsaid even today, more than twenty years later. The sense of abandonment (felt by both the local Detroit and national black communities) was exacerbated when Gordy sold Motown in 1988 to Boston Ventures for $61 million (without the Jobete music publishing catalogue). Motown was sold again in 1993 to Polygram for $301 million, a sale that included 30 artists, the most valuable of whom is Boyz II Men, and a catalogue of 30,000 master recordings. Gordy remains the chairman of the company.

Gordy left to black Detroit what was to become the museum (1987), which Michigan made an historical landmark in 1988—a combined tourist trap and institutionalized set of memories like Graceland, operating on a particularly impassioned nostalgia that the merchants of popular culture strive to induce in nearly everyone about his or her youth.

I first visited the Museum at the time of the second annual tribute to Marvin Gaye, which appears to be the museum's annual fund-raiser, entitled "What's Going On?" The tribute was held at Clubland on April 2, 1991, Gaye's birthday, but as Gaye suffered the misfortune of having been murdered by his father in 1984 on April 1, it was difficult to tell what was being commemorated. As Eliot wrote, "[W]ere we led all that way/for Birth or Death?" Smokey Robinson flew in to host a fairly inept affair. At first, the winners of an essay contest were announced; it was apparently open only to the senior class students of Cass Technical High School (a school Gaye did not attend since he grew up in Washington, D.C., not Detroit). The topic was "What's Going On . . . How Do We Make a Better Community, a Better World?" Just the sort of grandiose topic that makes a gesture toward social relevance and political awareness as it blunts the most remote possibility of producing either good writing or coherent thought. The winners were all girls which, surely, induced some in the audience to lament a favorite refrain these days: Where Have All the Young Black Men Gone? . . . Dead and Buried, Every One—so we are led to believe, and perhaps it is true. Once this portion of the show was stumbled through, it staggered into the musical performances, with various acts that ranged from amateurish to boring. The Contours, the main act and an old-time Motown group, was an intriguing finale. They performed their two major hits, "First I Look at the Purse" and "Do You Love Me (Now That I

Can Dance)?" but they also performed a kind of truncated history of 1960s soul: The Righteous Brothers' "You Lost That Loving Feeling" and two songs by Sam and Dave, "Hold On, I'm Coming" and "Soul Man," the Contours wound up subsuming two major aspects of 1960s pop music—blue-eyed soul and Issac Hayes/David Porter Stax soul—into a Motown mosaic. There was something disheartening about this compression of cultural history into a parodic medley by tired, middle-aged men.

The tribute focused mostly on Gaye's "What's Going On?"—the 1971 hit album that Gordy at first did not wish to release, thinking it to be, in the words of a true pop-music mogul, "insufficiently commercial." I am not sure if the tribute every year will be called "What's Going On?" yet there hardly seems another appropriate name for it from Gaye's music that could signify a kind of dignified social consciousness that black fund-raising events these days, as in days past, must have. Uplift must never be far from the minds of people who, in the end, either are not thinking seriously about it anyway and just using it as a way to bring black people together or are thinking of absolutely nothing else and so are constantly overwhelmed by the utter impossibility of ever bringing black people together.

"What's Going On?" is probably the greatest, most storied album that Motown ever released, far more sophisticated as a concept album than what the company previously issued, such as Christmas LPs and records like "A Bit of Liverpool" by the Supremes or "Tribute to Nat King Cole" by Gaye. In a series of striking and dramatic mood-music arias, Gaye, through admittedly banal lyrics—conveniently printed on the gatelike album cover as was the custom of the day so that songwriters might appear to be poets and albums might take on the resonance of a book—provides a black Christian vision of despair in a world of war, drug addiction, environmental abuses, and racism. (The musical antecedents of this album include Pharoah Sander's "Karma," John Coltrane's "A Love Supreme" and the mid-sixties protest songs of Oscar Brown, Jr. and Nina Simone.) What is most notable about this album in the Gaye *oeuvre* is its *sui generis* quality; he made no record like it before and, with the exception of some suggestion of pop political consciousness on his soundtrack LP, "Trouble Man," made no record like it after. His music, otherwise, was consumed and subsumed by sex, an image and direction that both distressed and delighted the disturbed and drug-addicted singer throughout his career. ("Baby, please don't hesitate or I may have to masturbate" are the fade-out lyrics on "Sexual Healing," his last big hit single.) Yet "What's Going On?" is a perfectly realized piece in Gaye's total vision, and the reason the album remains so beloved among blacks is that Gaye is clearly playing the role of the seer (even if his vision may have been partly drug-induced, as it is reported that he consumed "mountains of cocaine" in order to keep up his muse to complete the album). It is a jeremiad. On the cover we see a well-dressed, bearded Gaye—the first time he was shown with a beard, a cogent dismissal of his hope to become a mainstream crooner—standing in the rain, apparently on the grounds of his home. There is a swing set in the background. He has a concerned, even troubled look, the look of a prophet. Just as commentators have suggested that only through sexual metaphor can the Christian vision be made plain and intelligible to its believers, so Gaye subconsciously believed that the social vision of a miscegenated culture can only be made plain through sexual metaphor, through the yearning for union, which is what all pop sex songs are about. On the inner part of the cover of "What's Going On?" we see the social result of that union, the family, which is celebrated with a montage of scrapbooklike photos, where the Christian vision and the vision of black unity can meld—photos all the more strange because Gaye's home life as a child in his father's house and as a married man was so unhappy (he was married, at one time to Gordy's sister Anna). The album was simply a bridge from Gaye, the 1960s "fella" who posed innocently as a sexual object for women, to Gaye in the 1970s, the middle-aged sexual gaucho who fears impotency.

"Funny," Gaye once said, "but of all the acts back then [the 1960s], I thought Martha and the Vandellas came closest to really saying something. It wasn't a conscious thing, but when they sang numbers like 'Quicksand' or 'Wild One' or 'Nowhere To Run' or 'Dancing in the Street,' they captured a spirit that felt political to me. I liked that. I wondered to myself, with the world exploding around me, how am I supposed to keep singing love songs?" But like Countee Cullen, another black artist torn by his Christian and pagan (sexual) inclinations (and another black artist reared by a seemingly homosexual or transvestite black father who was a minister), Gaye the seer never was of a divided mind. He always saw the world through Christian lenses whether he was singing about sex or politics; indeed, for Gaye as a Christian and as an American black male, sex was indistinguishable from politics and from religion.

But central to Gaye's vision in "What's Going On?" is the father. The album cover depicts Gaye as father figure, as patriarch, in a sense, and in the songs he cries out to his Father (God) and to all fathers to recognize their sons. David Ritz, Gaye's biographer, is right to locate Gaye's torment in his hatred of his father (a minister who was a wife beater and a child abuser, according to Ritz), whose love Gaye desired but found impossible to obtain and, in some measure, repulsive to contemplate. Gaye sought other father figures in his career: Harvey Fuqua of the Moonglows, his first professional secular group, "Pops" Gordy, who once stopped Gaye from committing suicide, and Berry Gordy himself, who never completely understood his moody but most prized male singer. But Gaye was never reconciled to his real father. There remained only the intense hatred of a father who wanted his drug-addicted son dead and a son who wanted his drunken, cruel father dead: another instance of the expendability of black males through their self-hatred. They hated each other so much because they so deeply loathed themselves and what each saw of himself in the other.

The tribute survived and succeeded, such as it did, on the evocation of memory; it may be that as a political art "What's Going On?" is still vital today, but we are not sure if that is the case or if it is the memory of what had been vitality that makes it vital still. In Robert Townsend's film tribute to R and B, *The Five Heartbeats,* which was in the theaters at the time of my visit to Detroit, we have an almost unbearable, if at times, clumsy and inartistic claim made to memory and to fathers. It is about a group that seems to collapse our memories of 1950s groups—like Lee Andrews and the Hearts, the Marcels (a tribute to black processed hair?), the Flamingoes, the Ravens, and James "Shep" Sheppard and the Heartbeats themselves—with 1960s groups like the Temptations, the Four Tops, and the Stylistics; the Dells, a group popular in the 1950s, 1960s, and 1970s were technical advisors. The film opens with Robert Townsend's character remembering the history of the group, and perhaps for blacks in particular, this need for memory is more intense now than ever, when the group feels its identity is embattled and its position as a people compromised and diminished in American culture in more insidious ways than since the days of slavery. But this film, which is more a sentimental tribute to black male bonding than about music, fails because it does not focus on the need of and for tradition to be dramatized and acted out within the black community, so, in effect, it provides black folk with memory without history, with art without some sense of that which makes it art and makes it meaningful for the persons who make it and for whom it is made. In this conflict between fathers and sons, which drives the plot of the film, the fathers or authority figures—the group's manager, the evil record-company owner, the nay-saying father of the lead singer, the disapproving minister-father of one of the back-ground singers—are all either killed or forgotten in the end, with the exception of the minister-father who is falsely rejoined with his son without a dramatic moment for the viewer to understand how this took place. (Unlike *Sparkle,* made in 1976, and a far more wretched movie about an all-girl group, *The Five Heartbeats* in effect closes with the black church instead of opening with it. The church is not where the singers come from but it is what they go back to, a far more powerful, middle-brow message to black folk.) The guys in the group never talk about other singers they admire, other groups—especially gospel groups and sophisticated semijazz singers like the Ink Spots and the Mills Brothers who were the main source of inspiration for these doo-wop teen combos—from whom they stole riffs or ideas. Without this articulated bridge of artistic tradition in the black community, without this liaison between fathers and sons being stated explicitly, the film's family-reunion ending is worse than dishonest; it is utter and cruel deceit, pandering to an audience in the most obvious and cheap way, because the union has not been *earned,* it has only been *earnestly desired.* Like Gaye's "What's Going On?" *The Five Heartbeats* is a jeremiad that never becomes or wants to become a jeremiad but wishes its audience to believe that it is. Townsend's film never locates real memory for blacks. It captures only the barest echo of the vitality of pop cultural memory or art. Although Townsend wishes very much to have his characters transcend the very purpose that brought them together, in the end the only authenticity of this fictive family called the Five Heartbeats lies, alas, in its commercial power and charisma. Yet the film has a certain charm for the African-American mind even in its imperfections because the emotions it evokes are emotions that only blacks, not just anyone who remembers the earlier days of Rock and Roll, can feel. In this sense, it creates a certain middle-brow power because it creates a purely black nostalgia.

Townsend's fixation on fathers brings to mind the well-regarded 1964 film *Nothing But a Man,* about a young southern black man (Ivan Dixon) and his wife (Abbey Lincoln) trying to make it in the South of the early 1960s, shot in an almost documentary style by two white filmmakers, Robert Young and Michael Roemer. The films, in truth, have nothing in common except the theme of black fatherhood and, by extension, black manhood, as well as, in different ways, evoking Motown to create a sense of memory and community. In *Nothing*

But a Man, Motown music is used as the soundtrack, thus connecting Motown with what many critics and viewers, both black and white, feel to be the most politically and artistically well-wrought black film of the post–World War II era, clearly the black lower-class and middle-brow aspiration of the assertion of black manhood and the protection of the black family. That is why, I suppose, the film was rumored to be a favorite of Malcolm X who most vigorously spoke up for an assertive black manhood and protection of the black family in the early 1960s. *Nothing But a Man* is also obsessed with the redemption of the black father, as by film's end Dixon claims his son by another woman and brings him home, reunifying his precarious marriage with Abbey Lincoln. As Gloria Foster says in the film upon the death of Dixon's father, "I know he wasn't much of a father." To which Dixon cynically responds, "Who is?" If Townsend's film suggests that the black male is framed within the community of the nightclub, church, and the family (the opening, penultimate, and final shots in the film), then the earlier *Nothing But a Man* suggests that the black man is not truly framed by his community at all, but framed by both trains and cars, symbols of industry and mobility, framed either by the community that provides work on the trains or by the lack of community that the car offers as an escape. In this sense, despite the brilliance of *Nothing But a Man* and the manipulative ineptitude of *The Five Heartbeats,* the latter is the more important work. In the Townsend film, for instance, the black preacher as middle-brow conservator of blackness and compromised resistor to whites is far better understood, if less vividly depicted than the middle-class black preacher in *Nothing But a Man,* who is, Marxist style, just a sellout and an Uncle Tom. Yet *Nothing But a Man* was made during the early 1960s when black southern churches were being bombed because of their political activity or threat of political activity. In fact, more of these churches were bombed by terrorists during those years than any other American institution, sacred or secular, was ever attacked by terrorists in the history of the republic. In *Nothing But a Man* blacks can find neither true community nor solace in virtually anything. It is either struggle or escape, a vision that resembles that of the great southern and urban black writer Richard Wright, which has a compelling power but not a sense of completeness.

Perhaps Americans, black and white, are discomfited by our popular music because it seems to serve no great ends except to make money and to provide momentary diversion. Perhaps whites are discomfited because so much of our popular music, from ragtime to New Jack Swing, from jazz to hip-hop, has been called by slang terms derived from its rhythm (ragtime, swing, Rhythm and Blues, disco) or by slang terms for copulation (jazz and Rock and Roll), a fact that is discomfiting to some African-Americans as well. Perhaps blacks are discomfited because they cannot find in the African-American origins of American music a high and lofty object, an aspiration to artistic greatness and discipline that does not seem shaded by ambivalence. Perhaps we black folk sometimes do not like the entrapment of sensuality we are forced to wear as a mask for the white imagination. Yet there is in that sensuality an expression of holiness about the wonder of the union of like and unlike things. Everything is sexual, after all, and everything seeks marriage. American popular music thumbs its nose at the respectability of art while yearning for nothing but that respectability. This contradiction is the source of its strengths, and of its imbecility, its cheapness, its nonsense, its incivility, its disregard of taste. This contradiction is the source of our democratic possibilities in art.

But music has many objectives, serves many ends. And the story of American popular music is the story of American democracy at its best and its worst, a full revelation (in Ralph Ellison's words) of America's "rich diversity and its almost magical fluidity and freedom" as well as its "inequalities and brutalities." We have had over thirty-five years of *recognized* integrated national experience in this country, and in that period the success of Motown stands as the most shining hour of the American black in popular culture. Visiting the Motown Museum, attending the Marvin Gaye tribute, watching the Townsend film, listening again to the records, one is struck by the extent to which the memory of Motown, and more generally of its era, may be holding American blacks together, as we are torn apart by centrifugal social and political forces that frighten us even as they may, in the long run, bless us with a newer freedom. In the dangerous business of judging American popular art, certainly, it is difficult to tell what was Armageddon and what was just a teleological passing fancy.